The Idea Invaders

The Idea Invaders

by

GEORGE N. GORDON

IRVING FALK

WILLIAM HODAPP

COMMUNICATION ARTS BOOKS

HASTINGS HOUSE, PUBLISHERS

New York 22

To the "idea invaders":
May their invasion by truth
set us all free.

Published simultaneously in Canada by
S. J. Reginald Saunders, Publishers, Toronto 2B

Library of Congress Catalog Card Number: 63–13563
Printed in the United States of America

CONTENTS

From *The New York Times*, May 26, 1962

GENEVA, May 25 (Reuters)

—Following is the text of the Declaration Against War Propaganda submitted by the United States and the Soviet Union to the disarmament conference here today . . .

Convinced that the younger generation of today should be brought up in the spirit of peace, mutual respect and understanding among peoples:

Determined to promote by every means at their disposal friendly relations among states . . .

Recognizing that war propaganda in whatsoever form or country conducted which can provoke or encourage a threat to, or breach of, the peace . . .

Recognizing that an end to such propaganda could facilitate the conclusion of an agreement on general and complete disarmament:

1. Solemnly affirm their . . . condemnation of "all forms of propaganda, in whatsoever country conducted, which is either designed or likely to provoke or encourage any threat to the peace, or act of aggression":

2. Condemn appeals for war and for the settlement of disputes between states by the use of force, and also statements to the effect that war is necessary and inevitable:

3. Affirm their conviction that in our day, war can no longer serve as a method of settling international disputes and their desire to educate the younger generation in this conviction and to promote the ideas of peace, mutual respect and understanding among peoples:

4. Undertake to promote by every means at their disposal the widest possible circulation of news, ideas and opinions conducive to the strengthening of peace and friendship among peoples, and to extend cultural, scientific and educational reactions with a view to better dissemination of the ideas of peaceful and friendly cooperation among states, and general and complete disarmament.

AUTHORS' NOTE

MOUNTAINS of data went into the preparation of this volume; where possible, citations are included. Some of the information herein is derived, however, from confidential sources; some of the individuals interviewed asked that they not be quoted directly, or that they not be credited specifically; their requests have, of course, been honored. A few of the ancedotes used for illustration found their way to the authors by second-hand routes. They may well be apocryphal, but if they did not happen, perhaps they should have happened, and they are used for demonstration purposes only.

So many people have helped the authors in their quest that to list them here would look like vanity, or lead the reader to suppose that the book was written by a committee. We have thanked those who merit open thanks in the notes to each chapter (collected in the section beginning on page 233). It remains here only to observe that, with one or two exceptions, the degree of cooperation the authors received from private individuals and agencies as well as government employees, Congressmen, and other busy individuals was little short of amazing—as was the candor and honesty of most of them.

We should like only to single out Russell F. Neale of Hastings House, who gathered the threads of a number of ideas into this one; Theodore A. Dunst, whose editorial acumen provided a fresh viewpoint and clarification of certain aspects of the work; and Mary Darnell, Mina Shulman, Ellyn Thieberg, and the others who did the dirty work at the typewriter.

Gratitude notwithstanding, be warned that the authors will take full responsibility for any and all errors that appear on the pages that follow.

New York City, March 1, 1963

THE IDEA INVADER AND HIS TASK

Nature is as inimical to man as it is friendly . . . we see . . . that man is a stranger in a world he did not make, that nature is indifferent to us, that there is no natural power which has but to be learned in order to make us perfectly happy. Wouldn't it be terrible, we cry today, if atomic warfare wiped out the human race? There is no reason . . . to think so. If nature has purposes, we cannot know them; certainly there is no reason to think those purposes are directed to our benefit.

—MORSE PECKHAM in *Beyond the Tragic Vision*

INTRODUCTION

IDEAS can be inert thoughts, speculations, dreams; they can be spurs to action, fuses for dynamite.

The latter kinds of ideas are those which are the concern of this book. In its pages we have attempted to demonstrate how ideas with a purpose, spread by men with missions, have influenced the destinies of nations and the lives of individuals throughout history and at the present instant.

If this book has a moral, it is the simple fact that the most important things each of us possesses, the freedom of our minds and spirits—in short, the things that make life worth living—are at the mercy of the force of such ideas and of men with such missions.

At first blush, this is a book about propaganda and propagandists, and then it is much more. It is also a book about survival—the survival of free inquiry, free thought, and the free spirit, and possibly the survival of *all* our present civilizations. This is because propaganda has become, in our time, a life-or-death matter.

Of course, spears, guns, and hydrogen bombs are the instruments which do the real damage; talk is just talk. But we use our weapons *because* we have talked or *failed* to talk; *because* nations have communicated, one with the other, or *because* they have failed to communicate.

Perhaps the wisest thought of the twentieth century is the recognition that wars are made in the minds of men and that, if we are to achieve peace, this too must be constructed in the minds of men.

But how? Why is it so difficult for men to live at peace with one another? What is it about freedom that some men have so assiduously tried to smother it? What is it about truth that some men seek to smother the spontaneous pursuit of it?

Three factors distinguish our era from times past, and each of them relates intimately to the quality of the future, be it a future of peace or oblivion. Each is a challenge with which our century must grapple, and unless we face up to the problems they present, the year 2,000 will see a tranquillity without life that the face of this planet has not known for millions of years. Succinctly stated, they are:

1. The concept of total warfare
2. The concept of political self-determination
3. The concept of global prosperity

They are all revolutionary ideas. Had they been espoused a hundred years ago, they would have been considered symptoms of madness—in fact, they were so considered when one or another fell from the lips of nineteenth-century social dreamers like Henry George and Charles Fourier. Today they are realities to be reckoned with and our very salvation depends upon the way our statesmen, diplomats, and politicians are capable of dealing with them in the practical conduct of international affairs.

Taken together, the significance of these three concepts derives from the fact that our era is a period of common denominators of aspiration for all people on earth—and a period of common fear as well. Such a community has never before in history been known, but it is upon us now, this minute, and must be reckoned with.

We are *all* afraid of destruction. We have *all* awakened to the fact that power flows from the governed to the ruler and not the other way around. We *all* know that human society can provide enough food and material goods to feed, clothe, and house every person on earth and even produce a surplus.

Equally important is the knowledge that all of us in the free world should share the fact that our fundamental traditions and freedoms are also in peril of being lost, not necessarily in a mushroom of radioactive atmosphere, but by our default and out of our apathy in a blast of words from the mouths of idea invaders who speak for the enemies of our deepest beliefs. These are the men who have caused us to coin the term "menticide" to describe the process by which the mind is reduced to see all history, all life, and all of man's endeavors as mere functions of determinisms held as dogmas.

Our awareness of these threats taken together makes us different from the people who have preceded us on earth. We who are citizens of the United States have a particularly fearful responsibility in regard to them because, for much of the world, it will be *our* philosophies of life, *our* foreign policies, and the actions of *our* statesmen which will determine how the political, economic, and military future unfolds, not only in the United States but in the furthest corners of the globe.

This is where propaganda enters the picture.

The main task of the idea invader of the free nations today is to clarify for the rank and file of the world the nature of the military, political, economic and cultural changes through which that world—on both sides of the Iron Curtain—is moving. All other objectives for mass persuasion are secondary, corollary, and of little pith or moment.

Whatever the method we choose, the task is the same: to prepare every man on earth to live in a century of self-government, economic prosperity, and peace. That the Soviet Union has taken the route of Marxist pseudo-science and (temporarily, it claims) political tyranny, that it uses imperialistic techniques to condemn imperialism, and that it has permitted a tradition of Russian despotism to color its conduct in the international arena, is unfortunate. That it has chosen to stifle freedom of inquiry and of the right to dissent in favor of a construction of history which sees man, not as Godlike in stature, but rather as the pawn of elemental economic conflicts, is no less than tragic.

The nature of the USSR's *modus vivendi* does not alter the basic challenge it also faces, any more than our capitalism, democratic idealism, or traditions alter ours. The objective is the same: to create a social and political climate the world over where men can live decent lives, share equitably what they produce, and achieve, each one, his potential to develop his unique, individual personality.

This is the main role mass persuasion has to play in this last part of the twentieth century.

Many diversions along the way, however, face the free world's idea invader. He must grapple with a cold war and the competition his opposite number on the other side of the Iron Curtain is giving him. He must face an unsettled political picture in South America, Africa, and Asia. He must balance the aspirations of backward nations with traditional hostilities, economic realities, and military expediencies.

In times of crises, the world he faces is, in short, chaotic, seemingly millions of light years away from the ideal of safety, peace, prosperity. He is like Shaw's Don Juan, seeking truth but finding only hostility, corruption, and hypocrisy wherever he goes, and forced, as a final choice, to hell, where at least honesty reigns.

Let the idea invader take heart, however. This is his century, and he is one of the most important men living in it.

His voice may be the herald of the future. In the distressing term of public relations expert Edward Bernays, he is the "engineer of consent," who will pave the way for the world a'coming, whatever it holds. And he may even have the power to help to shape that world into a decent place to live. What could be more important than that?

This book is about the power of ideas and about the idea invaders themselves.

Who are they? Any and all people who write, speak, make films, television and radio shows, or what-not for the purpose of persuasion.

There are idea invaders whose objectives are relatively trivial: to persuade us to buy a chocolate bar or not to throw trash on subway platforms. This book will not be concerned with them; they have received more than their share of literary attention in recent years.

The idea invaders we shall center on will be those whose ideas are *universal,* that is, those concerned with concepts of political, social, or historical value. If you wish, this book deals mostly with "international propaganda," but to confine its limit to so narrow a term misreads its intent and nature. Its range covers a host of new frontiers in mass communication in many dimensions.

We shall discuss, in Part I, the historical context into which mass persuasion fits today. By observing the great propagandists of the past, and by means of a close-up of German and Russian propaganda history, we shall set the scene for a description of the idea invaders of the present. Part II concerns the many and informal influences on the minds of foreigners exerted by the United States—our mass media, our tourists abroad, our business men—stopping along the way (in Chapter 4) for a case study of how the process works. In Part III, we focus on how official and semi-official persuasion does and might occur at the hands of our advertisers, philanthropists, and government agencies. The book concludes with a chapter which discusses the "image" of America.

PART ONE

THE MASS PERSUADERS

PROPAGANDA'S PAST

In the beginning was the Word.

—St. John II

Speech is civilization itself. The word, even the most contra-dictory word, preserves contact—it is silence which isolates.

—Thomas Mann in *The Magic Mountain*

Public sentiment is everything; with public sentiment, nothing can fail; without it, nothing can succeed. . . . He who moulds opinion is greater than he who enacts law.

—Abraham Lincoln

CHAPTER 1

THIS is the story of *mass persuasion.* It begins as far back as recorded history itself. It is a story of the attempts to recognize the minds and hearts of various sorts of publics and hence to understand their behaviors.

Many of the Biblical prophets, Joshua among them, rank as persuaders of the first order. William Albig[1] notes that Herodotus, upon whom the modern world largely depends for its pictures of the ancient world, utilized propaganda for the Athenian state. Indeed, this seems highly likely, since "the father of history" was a political type, and it is not unlikely that he was even a professional civil servant of Athens, having helped found the Athenian colony of Thurii in Italy. It is not difficult, therefore, to understand why history has so clearly demarcated the "good guys" and the "bad guys" in the 49-year conflict called the Persian Wars. Since the dispute was covered for posterity by a devout Athenian, neither the Persian Darius nor his son Xerxes stood much of a chance of passing through history as heroes.

There is little question that the philosopher Plato was also, strictly speaking, a political propagandist. In *The Republic*

17

he idealized the perfect state, one governed by the philosopher-kings, and from it he excluded all those who might lead the citizenry away from rationality and clear thought. Specifically, he meant the poets and the singers of songs. His political model no doubt was meant to persuade political factions in real life to adopt the policies it espoused. They did—and Plato's influence is felt to this day in the way many modern governments are administered.

An interesting sidelight on Plato's distrust of the arts and artists is that the artist himself has always been something of a mass persuader, appealing to the emotions on a collective basis. The artist has mastered the techniques of the mass manipulator, and legislators, leaders of state, and philosophers throughout history have therefore frequently attempted to proscribe the arts, since they can become instruments for managing public opinion. Or they have *used* the arts to pacify the people as did the Roman emperors who gave the public bread and circuses in order that the citizen, his stomach filled and his eye dazzled, be diverted from the cares of state and the machinations of the legislators. It is no wonder that sports arenas, circus tents, festivals, fairs, pageants, parades, pomp, splendor, and ceremony have all been used in the long story of civilization as means and techniques for the manipulation of public opinion, as they are used today all over the world in both open and closed societies.

The Roman state knew other kinds of propagandists as well. Caesar's diaries, Cicero's oratory, Marcus Aurelius' political writing, all contain elements found today in modern propaganda, and all were designed, in one degree or another, to manage "public opinion," or at least the opinions of that part of the public involved in political matters.

In fact, it is unlikely that any revolutionary activity or any vast changes in accepted orders in history were not accompanied by some kind of psychological warfare. During the American Revolution, Sam Adams pamphleteered, influenced, persuaded. In staging the Boston Tea Party, Adams demonstrated the value of created events to dramatize a political point of view in terms of action of symbolic importance, a technique which has been used frequently throughout history. Benjamin Franklin wrote, talked, and convinced prominent individuals to support the rebel cause both at home and abroad. Thomas Paine possessed something of a genius for this art. Over 100,000 copies of his pamphlet *Common Sense* were sold within three months after its publication in January, 1776. In *The Crisis* he wrote, "These are the times that try men's souls. The summer soldier and the sunshine patriot will, in this crisis, shrink from the service of their country; but he that stands it *now,* deserves the love and thanks of man and woman. Tyranny, like hell, is not easily conquered." [2] And his words still ring to this day with his two-fisted determination.

At the time of the French Revolution soldiers were dispatched into battle reciting slogans such as, "War to the fancy houses; peace for thatched cottages!" and the like. Robespierre let it be known that the Revolution was not only a blow for the independence of France but an international upheaval concerned with the rights of man everywhere. So intensive was this propaganda gambit that the British king objected to it as a violation of international law which the French Constitution eventually recognized.[3]

The actual word "propaganda" probably had its origins in the history of the Catholic Church. During the period that the Church was, in fact, "catholic" in Europe—that is, before the Protestant heresy—there was little need to convince anyone that the road to Rome was the true and exclusive road to salvation. Occasional heretics like Savonarola in the fifteenth century usually found their impact disappearing in the long run. But the Reformation was something else again, and, with the invention of printing at about the time that America was discovered, heretical ideas could be spread quickly, cheaply, and effectively. It was then high time for the Church to protect its interests.

In 1622 Pope Gregory XV organized the College of Propaganda, whose function was the propagation of faith. It was supposed to supervise liturgical books and instruct clerics on methods of proselytizing for the faith. It was also, where the interests of Rome were involved, not beyond attempting to use certain types of political persuasion.[4]

Modern propaganda—both national and international—rose to dimensions of significance with three vital changes in the Western (and now Eastern) world, all of which heightened to meaningful dimensions the power of persuasion for good or for evil.

First came the invention of the means of *mass* communications. This meant the cheap and effective spread of words and images to more people than ever before in history. And, as each medium of communication was perfected and mass-produced—from printing to film to radio to television—this mass audience increased apace.

Second, from the beginning of the nineteenth century onward (a by-product of the democratic ideal of free, universal education), larger and larger numbers of people were learning to *read*—at least to read enough to constitute a fair target for the man with a message if his medium of communication was the printed word.

Third, and also as a corollary of democratic idealism, people *en masse* became increasingly important as instruments of political activity, both national and international, and public opinion became more and more a vital factor in political and diplomatic maneuvers. It mattered not a bit what the medieval serf thought on any particular issue; he was politically inert, impotent to change the forces which governed his life in terms of both national and international issues. When the serf was educated and given political power by means of the vote and taught the equalitarian ideals of democracy, it *did* matter crucially what he thought, and there was more than likely to be someone around who attempted to manage his thinking for him.

The history of propaganda has also produced various individuals of color and significance as they figure in the history of the West. None is more fascinating in his life and career than the man who, more than any other thinker, saw the power and devised the methods by which mass persuasion could be accomplished, even though he was writing long before the modern revolution in mass communications was to increase the traveling speed of the trouble-makers he released from Pandora's box.

His name is Niccolo Machiavelli,[5] the famous Florentine, who was born in 1469, was educated in the classics, and managed to become a Renaissance political bigwig. Owing to the caprices of fate, he was exiled from his native city in 1512, and having suffered imprisonment and torture, he thought to curry favor with the second Lorenzo di Medici by composing a little book he called *The Prince,* in which he set down some hard-boiled principles on how to be a ruler for fun and profit. It is doubtful whether Lorenzo ever got to see the document, and it was not published until five years after Machiavelli's death. But the book's influence up to the present moment on the literature of politics and mass persuasion has been extensive. It is doubtful whether one despot, benevolent or otherwise, since its publication has not profited from Machiavelli's observations. In the world of letters, the very term "Machiavellian" pertains to a clever schemer or manipulator. Shakespeare, for instance, was influenced by him to the extent that the character Iago was patterned after the Florentine himself, and to this day the "fine Italian hand" about which we speak is Niccolo's.

What the document says, and what makes it a handbook for the mass persuader, is less its emphasis on the tricks of government and propaganda and more its statement of morality. Machiavelli, as noted by Princeton's famous teacher and counselor Christian Gauss,[6] sees the state as a *force* for good or evil and the citizen as an *object* of manipulation; public opinion is seen as malleable, capable of control by the clever leader who, in the exercise of his power, is able to achieve a common assent in order to steer the ship of state judiciously. According to Machiavelli, the devices which a Prince employs, the good and evil of means, are less important than the worthiness of ends.

Contrary to popular fancy, Machiavelli by no means exalted villainy for its own sake. His ideas were detached from considerations of villainy or virtue: he was interested in what *worked,* and the tricks of the trade about which he speaks were probably pretty accurate descriptions of how rulers like the Medici and the Borgias *did* operate and how they kept their power so long. Nonetheless, Machiavelli had considerable admiration for leaders like the ruthless Cesare Borgia. He commended the latter's proclivity for appointing his friends to high positions, pretending friendship toward those he hated and turning against former friends when necessary. The important thing, to Machiavelli, was that the ruler *appear to be* beyond reproach, a repository of virtue and goodness no matter what transgressions were necessary for the good of the state. This, of course, is the cardinal rule of this kind of skillful propagandist if he has any prayer of being accepted by his audience.

While Machiavelli was dreaming up a handbook for the manipulator in Italy, another ingenious gentleman was using similar devices in England.[7] Sir Thomas More, subject of Robert Bolt's play, "A Man For All Seasons," known widely for his humanistic philosophy and for his authorship of *Utopia* (a dream of a superstate of absolute perfection and grace), was Chancellor to Henry VIII. Sir Thomas himself enjoyed little perfection or grace in Tudor England. He broke with Henry in 1532 and ended up on the execution block for treason in 1535 because he doubted Henry's right to take over the English Catholic Church. More is also a key figure in the history of propaganda.

While More was in the king's service, he was, wittingly or unwittingly, an expert propagandist. Henry, a headstrong individual who eventually broke with the Pope because of the latter's disapproval of his tendency to divorce women who could not bear him sons, was extraordinarily anxious to enhance the reputation of the then royal family. His father, Henry VII, had been the first Tudor king who came to power in the vacuum created by the conflict between the families of Lancaster and York in the fifteenth century. Henry VII's mortal enemy was Richard III, whom he vanquished in 1485 at the battle of Bosworth Field, where Shakespeare has Richard ready to sacrifice his "kingdom for a horse." Born a Lancaster, Henry VII settled the whole dispute between the two houses by marrying Elizabeth of York and founding the House of Tudor.

Henry VII's son, the impetuous—and clever—Henry VIII had a good reason, then, for desiring to hurl whatever discredit he could upon the memory of his father's one-time adversary, Richard III, and upon the House of York, to which his mother—but not his father—had once belonged. This move was well calculated to increase popular support of the

Tudors. From the pen of Sir Thomas More (or from a document found with his effects after he was dead and possibly planted there by the wily Henry) there emerged a book, the *History of Richard III,* in which the York king was portrayed as a wicked hunchback deformed in mind and body, a fiend responsible for the murder of his two young nephews in his greedy race to the British crown.

Nothing could be further from the truth, as many historians, Horace Walpole among them, have attested.[8] More was a child when Richard was in power and, no doubt with Henry VII's approval (or possibly on his orders), his "history" was sheer fabrication. It served as anti-York propaganda, probably based upon "information" given More by a curiously devious figure in British history, one John Morton, Archbishop of Canterbury to Henry VII and a devoted follower of the king. Morton hated Richard III and his family with a venom second only to that of Henry himself. Richard III's deviltry as portrayed in More's history is, therefore, patent hokum. Better sources than More's, contemporaneous with Richard III, indicate that he was a benign and benevolent monarch, not disfigured in any way, beloved by his subjects, and more sinned against than sinning.

This propaganda had its effect, however. William Shakespeare, writing a chronicle of English history in his plays (and incidentally, composing also at the pleasure of Elizabeth, Henry VIII's daughter and a Tudor to her toes), used More's history for the character of Richard III, and enforced this distortion of him and his career that history accepted. Propaganda had done its work and this is why encyclopedias to this day present as fact what was only a clever ruse, a bit of persuasion and idea invasion by a British king and his idea manipulators!

Modern propaganda also owes something of a debt to the eighteenth-century philosopher Jean Jacques Rousseau, who developed the term—and to a degree, the *idea*—of "public opinion" as the twentieth-century persuader reckons it. In his discussions of the *volante generale* or general will, Rousseau saw clearly that he who governs a modern state must do so with the consent of the governed if any semblance of modern liberal political thought is to displace the arbitrary despotisms of the past. He understood that achieving this consent required the clever manipulation of public opinion.

As we have noted, it was, of course, the invention of printing at the end of the fifteenth century which gave power to the ideas of men like Machiavelli and to the distortions in More's *History of Richard III*. As printing became cheaper, as new methods for the setting of type and the production, binding, and distribution of books were invented, and as literacy spread from the aristocracies down to the middle and lower classes both in Europe and America, so increased likewise the force and amount of propaganda to which people might be exposed.

In the nineteenth century a remarkable French psychologist added his mite to what we know about persuasion. Affirming Machiavelli's observation that people can be manipulated by good as well as evil forces, and that, from the manipulator's point of view, good and evil refer to ends rather than means, he carried this train of thought one step further. His name is Gustave Le Bon; his observations were quite simple but important for the history of mass persuasion and propaganda.[9]

In the first place Le Bon noticed that the behavior of people as *groups* or *crowds, audiences* or *publics,* was quite different from the individual behaviors of the persons who made up these collectives when observed singly. Second, he thought that the behavior of groups was more primitive, less elaborate, less civilized, and less inhibited by moral restraints than that of individuals. In the crowd, he observed an absence of restraint, a diminution of social controls, and a sense of irresponsibility. Third, he noticed that the crowd's behavior tended toward emotionality rather than reason, and that its responses were less rational than those of the average individual in it—a good deal more likely to call attention to the primitive sides of man's nature.

Le Bon's idea of the crowd was, of course, a mystique, and various thinkers have questioned its adequacy as social psychology—just as Machiavelli's ideas have been questioned as political theory. But as *observations* and, accordingly, as useful practical guides in manipulating masses, they were shrewd, practical, and efficient. Hitler, Mussolini, Lenin, and Stalin, we are told, were all close students of Le Bon. Theorists concerned with the art of propaganda have taken much from him also. The victim of mass persuasion is a part of "the crowd" as described by Le Bon even if he is isolated on a mountain top. Le Bon says, in effect, that appeals to the emotional nature of men are a good deal more likely to be acted upon than appeals to their rational side.

Considering Le Bon's observations, it is not strange that in the slogans of Nazi Germany, Fascist Italy, and other authoritarian states in which power was held irrelevantly to the will of the people, fanaticism, and unreasoning worship of the state and the leader are dominant themes of the party line. In totalitarian nations, thought is not required of the good citizen. To think means to deflate the emotional hypnosis, to destroy the crowd effect of which Le Bon speaks and upon which demagogues depend for the manipulation of public opinion.

Thus also does the propagandist, in an attempt to appeal to emotions, humanize and personalize abstract issues and even the very concept of the state. He endeavors to give it an image of warmth, of compassion and human dimensions—Mother Russia, Uncle Sam, and John Bull, for instance—in order that loyalty will be a matter of tenacious emotional involvement rather than the rational choice which may be vulnerable to doubts and arguments.

Modern propaganda, as we are exposed to it today, dates from the invention of modern methods of mass communication—the late nineteenth century for the film, the late teens and early twenties for radio, the forties and fifties for television.[10] Germany used wireless communication to spread distorted news bulletins during World War I; the Allies broadcast as well, spreading wide the news of Wilson's Fourteen Points to friends and foes. The Russian Bolsheviks also protested, by means of radio, the terms of the Brest-Litovsk peace treaty in an attempt to arouse popular opinion as pressure on German negotiators. The Hungarian Communist, Bela Kun, shortly after World War I was so effective in broadcasting his propaganda messages around the world that official protests against his talks were heard from Switzerland and Austria.

As we shall see, the leaders of the Soviet Union in the nineteen-twenties started idea invasion by means of radio in peacetime, broadcasting, without permission of the various countries to which their programs were beamed, in the language of the nations they were addressing. Great Britain, too, began its famous Empire Service in 1932, in part designed to serve as a link for colonials with London (Big Ben's chimes identified the service), but also as propaganda for British causes and interests.

The Netherlands began radio propaganda in 1927; France broadcast to her colonies in 1931; Hitler's international radio service began in 1933; German language programs originated from France in 1936; and by 1937 Italy was on the air in eighteen languages. Italy's programs included broadcasts in Arabic intended to stir up the Middle East against England and drew an official protest from the British. By 1938 the

English were beaming programs to Italy in Italian and to
Germany in German.

At the outbreak of World War II it was pretty well understood that warfare on the psychological fronts was equal in
importance (under certain circumstances) to warfare on the
military front. America also had to face the fact that she was a
late starter in the war for men's minds. Although we had attempted some broadcasting to South America before the war,
and RCA had an active international short-wave division in
the 1930's, we entered the field of international communications after 1941 well at the heels of the British, the Italians,
and the Germans. We had a lot to learn.

Our dilatory entrance into the struggle for the minds of
men was one more indication of our late retreat from isolation—political, economic, cultural, and military—from the
problems which other nations were facing and which by 1940
had reached global dimensions. As other kinds of isolation
yielded to the recognition of our interdependence with other
nations, so were we drawn into the arena of international
persuasion.

The conclusions we can draw from this brief history of
persuasion are as explicit as they are significant for our international future. In the first place the power of the propagandist, as Machiavelli demonstrated, is enormous—for better or
worse. He may use it for political purposes, to create climates
of opinion in which public assent can be assured for his policies even in future generations, as our look at Henry VIII and
Sir Thomas More revealed. His power is so great because he
can speak to men in their most brutal, uncivilized, and least
rational modes of behavior and, in the manner observed by
Le Bon, can exact from them their most primitive responses. It
is also true that propaganda today has become an arm of diplomacy, and every modern state is vigorously engaged in the in-

vasion of ideas. In the vacuum created by fear of atomic warfare, this war of words may therefore be the life-or-death struggle which determines in the end whether our way of life, our values, and our ideas of democracy will survive the twentieth century to be passed on to our children and grandchildren.

If the voices that speak across national boundaries are anything like the ones we shall listen to in the next chapter, if they have mastered the lessons taught by the great propagandists of the past with a fraction of his cleverness and skill, *and* if they imitate his ruthless, immoral disregard for human decency—and if we believe them blindly—the future is indeed bleak for us.

Now let us meet the devil at the microphone.

THE DEVIL AT THE MICROPHONE

If you wish the sympathy of broad masses, then you must tell them the crudest and most stupid things.

—ADOLPH HITLER

Propaganda has only one object—to conquer the masses. Every means that furthers this aim is good; every means that hinders it is bad. Success is its only criterion [italics supplied].

—PAUL JOSEPH GOEBBELS

CHAPTER **2**

THE most effective propagandists in history have been individuals who—to a man—have been intensely devoted and dedicated to the principles for which they used their wiles. One might expect from them a high degree of cynicism—superiority even—in regard to the tenets of their persuasion, since they themselves know best the devious soft spots in their manipulation. But no, their commitment is curiously subjective and complete, like that of the magician who believes secretly in black art despite his awareness that his own magic is mere sleight of hand.

Dr. Paul Joseph Goebbels, the main subject of this chapter, was just such a devoted, dedicated, intelligent, and resourceful man. Hitler's administration of Germany's Third Reich was composed, on the upper echelons, of men of such unexpectedly high intelligence,[1] and there is little question but that Goebbels was a star in Der Fuehrer's diadem when it came to propaganda genius.

His devotion, sincerity, and degree of commitment to the things he believed are also beyond question. In fact, he eventually demonstrated his faith in the ideals of the leader he adored so intensively in a most tangible way: on the evening of April 30, 1945, at shortly past 8:30 P.M. Berlin time after his wife, Magda, had administered lethal doses of poison to their six children, the Doctor shot his wife and subsequently put a bullet into his own brilliant brain. His body was discovered the following day by Russian troops who were in the process of occupying the city of Berlin. Feeble attempts to burn it—as the body of Hitler had previously been burned—had failed, and the final remains of this dedicated soul were buried beneath an unmarked grave.

Dr. Goebbels was indeed intelligent, dedicated, and sincere. He was also quite mad, a testament to the fact that madness may coexist with the widest assortment of conventional human virtues, a lesson that our century has not yet learned.

It is largely because of the Doctor and the application of his peculiar gifts to the promulgation of civilization's second most horrible madness of the past generation that the very word "propaganda" has an ugly ring to it today and why it is frequently euphemized into softer terms like "persuasion," "information," or "public relations." The imprint of Dr. Goebbels' hand still exudes from the term, and probably will for as long as he himself is remembered as the instrument of the devil that he was.

There is much that it is possible to learn from the careful study of even the most heinous beasts who have populated our planet. William Shirer quotes George Santayana at the beginning of his remarkable book, *The Rise and Fall of the Third Reich,* with the words, "Those who do not remember the past are condemned to relive it," and the particular past which Paul Joseph Goebbels stands for as a seminal figure is one that our race can ill afford to relive.

Any study of persuasion written today can ill afford, also, to ignore this creature, whose destructive intellect bulldozed the pathway down which Adolph Hitler ran so quickly to the mastery and subjugation of nearly all that was decent or civilized about Europe after World War I. Like it or not, he has contributed much to the understanding of mass persuasion in the modern world and, if this understanding yields some measure of defense against men of his stripe in the future, perhaps he has exculpated one measly fraction of evil he generated during his lifetime.

Let us look at the man:

He was born on October 29, 1897, into an exceedingly devout home; his parents were strict and pious Catholics, and, as Eric Hoffer has noted,[2] "the true believer believes truly." The context of his beliefs may change, but its intensity does not. Paul Joseph turned out in later life to be as devout as his parents, but his god was a psychopath with a Charlie Chaplin moustache.

Goebbels received an excellent German education. He attended parochial school, the *Gymnasium,* and eight universities including Heidelberg, from which he received a Ph.D. degree when he was twenty-four years old. His doctoral dissertation reflected his interests in history and literature and was concerned with the romantic drama. Illness and an operation as a child had crippled him, and in his adult life he walked with a limp; he was short, thin, and frail, but his energy and stamina were reflected in the profusion of novels, plays, and poems that came from him in his twenties (most of them unpublished and unproduced), and in his pursuit of the never-ending assortment of beautiful women with whom he had one affair after another—a proclivity which continued past his marriage to Magda Quandt in 1931 and the birth of his six children, and almost up until the end of his life.

In 1923 or 1924 he became involved with the Nazis—largely under the aegis of Karl Kaufmann and Gregor and Otto

Strasser, early enthusiasts of the movement—and he was employed as a sort of secretary, editor, and public speaker for the party. The Nazis had been an on-again, off-again political force—not taken very seriously by the German people—since 1920, when young Adolph Hitler, then twenty-one years old, retired as a painter of post-cards and anatomy illustrations for textbooks to devote full time to a design for living for Europe, and ultimately, so he thought, for the world.

By 1926 Goebbels and Hitler had begun the mutual admiration society that was to survive until their deaths. During the previous year, Goebbels' regard for the Communists had nettled Der Fuehrer, and he even denounced Hitler at a district party meeting in Hanover in 1925. One can imagine the degree of gorge this raised in the Fuehrer. But the two eventually kissed and made up (quite literally), and in 1926 Goebbels was appointed Nazi party Gauleiter of Berlin. When Hitler came to power in 1933, Paul Joseph Goebbels became his Propaganda Minister.

His concept of propaganda was essentially a simple one. It was unsophisticated and as crude as Hitler's idea of government, which the latter had characterized thus: "The Fuehrer is the Party and the Party is the Fuehrer—just as I feel myself only as a part of the Party, the Party feels itself only as a part of me."

Propaganda was, for Goebbels, an absolute, total enterprise. Its job was to enhance the welfare of the state, and this might affect the lives of the people. "I believe that when a propaganda ministry is created," he wrote, "all matters affecting propaganda, news and culture within the Reich and within the occupied areas must be subordinated to it. I emphasized [to Hitler] that I insist on totalitarianism in carrying out the propaganda and news policies of the Reich. He agreed with me absolutely and unreservedly." [3]

therefore always be essentially simple and repetitious. In the long run only he will achieve basic results [sic] in influencing public opinion who is able to reduce problems to the simplest terms and who has the courage to keep forever repeating them in this simplified form despite the objections of the intellectuals." [8]

This objective—the simple manipulation of people by primitive reasoning, slogans, and basic lies—was not difficult for Dr. Goebbels to achieve. In his private papers we see him ruminating about thought-control thus: "There are certain words from which we should shrink as the Devil does from holy water; among these are, for instance, the words 'sabotage' and 'assassination.' One must not permit such terms to become part and parcel of everyday usage." [9] We are given a vision of a totally unprincipled rascal who will not resist using the most unscrupulous means imaginable for his purposes, even to the absurd extreme of exploiting fortune-tellers and astrologers to give credence to his blatant idiocies.[10]

From the point of view of our interests, however, Nazi propaganda had an extremely severe limitation—a limitation which, possibly, saved the world from its incendiary and destructive tendencies. It is not a coincidence that this shortcoming had a direct parallel in the personality of Dr. Goebbels, as well as in the personality of his boss, Hitler.

The defect was that Nazi propaganda, like Goebbels himself, was unbelievably parochial. The basic views of both Hitler and Goebbels in this regard were quite naive. While their thought-control faced realistically the problem of controlling German society, culture, and values, it was less attractive overseas. As Manvell and Fraenkel state, "Over and over again, Goebbels showed his ignorance of the character of countries outside Germany, although he had the foreign press studied by his monitors." [11]

He tried hard, of course, to advance Germany's cause abroad. Building on the network of German embassies, he employed propaganda attachés at each, and continually dispatched instructions to them via diplomatic channels. An example of these orders (which leaked out to French newspapers) contains this paragraph: "To the outside world, all our propaganda must underline impressively that Germany does not wish for anything but a peaceful settlement of all pending problems. . . . In a skillful way all those who have refused to accede to Germany's rightful demands must be blamed for the failure of a peaceful understanding. . . . This must be done unobtrusively and in a constantly varying manner. . . . We must persuade at least part of public opinion abroad that Germany has no other way to take than what is absolutely coming to her. . . . Developments in our foreign policy which have already taken place as well as those which are about to take place make it imperative that the offices charged with propaganda and enlightenment concentrate their work in the immediate future more strongly on foreign countries." [12]

In addition to personnel in his embassies, Goebbels sent abroad business men, so-called journalists, and tourists, as well as representatives of pan-German organizations and various German friendship groups, to the extent that, in the relatively uneventful year of 1937, he managed to spend one hundred million dollars on this effort. Any and all Germans traveling overseas were given explicit instructions in persuasion techniques and in the best ways in which to hammer at the Nazi line of the moment, in a manner quite like the indoctrination given Soviet citizens who travel at present.

What was the extent and nature of the propaganda Dr. Goebbels directed against the United States, and why didn't it work—*or did it?* As we have noted, Goebbels was a severely narrow-minded man; his sights rarely extended beyond the territorial borders of Germany when it came to understanding political and social forces motivating other cultures of the world. Perhaps this naïveté explains why he even bothered with, and spent estimated millions of dollars on, propaganda for the USA in the first place. One tragic flaw in his personality—and in Hitler's also—was his tendency invariably to underestimate the abilities, stabilities, or determination of Americans. Nor could he, supreme egotist that he was, understand the depths of the hatred so many millions of Americans felt for him and everything the Nazi movement stood for. It was this blind spot that would eventually destroy him.

Attempt to influence the USA he did, however, and the study in some detail of exactly what he did or what he attempted to do is in order here if we are to come to a clear perception of what kinds of persuasion can and cannot succeed in the international arena. Both the successes and failures of Dr. Goebbels are highly relevant to *our* successes and failures in the years that followed as we attempted to speak to nations abroad.

Let us look at three aspects of this propaganda campaign: its administration and organization, the broadcasts beamed to the USA, and the propaganda themes which Dr. Goebbels hoped would either swing American sentiment to Germany's side and prevent us from entering World War II or, failing in this objective, undermine American morale and keep us from making our most determined and forceful efforts in the conflict.[13]

Section VII, or the Foreign Section of the Propaganda Ministry, administered Dr. Goebbels' overseas persuasion. How it worked can best be described in the words of Von Gienanth, Goebbels' propaganda attaché at the German Embassy in Washington, as he recently recounted his career. Said he, "My duties at the Embassy included all the same fields for which the Propaganda Ministry was responsible in Germany. First, political propaganda; second, film; third, literature; fourth, radio; fifth, press; sixth, music; seventh, art. . . . I accepted invitations to make speeches in universities and the like. I tried to get speakers to present the German cause. . . ." [14] Naturally, it was his job, also, to keep in touch with as many Nazi sympathizers in the United States as possible and offer them encouragement and, frequently, funds for their work.

The organizations which attempted to indoctrinate Americans into Nazism were many and widespread, including such quasi-governmental groups as the German Library of Information and the German Railroads Information Office, both located in New York City, and Transocean, the official German news agency and its competing organization, DNB. There was also the German-American Bund led by Fritz Kuhn and Gerhardt Wilhelm Kunze, a sort of marching and chowder society, which held rallies in Madison Square Garden in New York and on one occasion mustered as many as 22,000 Nazi sympathizers. Other less impressive groups, such as the Citizens' Committee to Keep America Out of War; We, the Mothers; and the like were vaguely sympathetic to the German cause and called themselves "isolationist."

Along with peripatetic propagandists like correspondent Karl H. Von Wiegand, who filed stories friendly to the Nazi cause from Germany, William Dudley Pelley and his "Silver Shirts," and George Sylvester Viereck, a long-term German propagandist and espionage agent, there were sympathetic assists from Americans who had been duped by Nazi doubletalk. A surprisingly large and well-organized nucleus existed here in America upon which Goebbels could hang the framework of his persuasion. In addition, Germany broadcast by radio nightly to the United States, and these programs, aside from their potential use as direct propaganda for the listener, also served to disseminate the themes, arguments, and over-all agenda for the individual propagandists in the United States who would "take it from there," spreading vitriol throughout America.

For this reason, the broadcasts were the heart and soul of the entire Nazi campaign, and constituted the prime link between Dr. Goebbels' boys in the United States and the home office. Of little concern to us is the fact that they were also loaded with information for espionage agents, saboteurs, and local Nazi strategists. Let us examine them only as persuasive instruments—mindful, of course, that in respect to this kind of propaganda, Dr. Goebbels was something of a trail-blazer, having few models for effective formats of international persuasion aside from some early attempts by Italy, Russia, and Great Britain.

The broadcasts themselves have been studied by propaganda experts in some detail,[15] and while they represented a wide range of program formats, it is interesting to follow the main tricks and devices they employed—tricks which were fully shifted around where dictated by political and military necessity.

First, the broadcasts displayed mainly a *negative* face. They attempted to undermine American faith in our institutions by attacking Wall Street, our allies, and our newspapers and radio networks. Our leaders, particularly President Roosevelt, were vilified, crises were exaggerated, and our anti-Germanism was ridiculed. As one broadcaster said sardonically, "Soon it will be time also for burning German textbooks and smashing German cameras and mouth organs. Patriotic mothers will refuse to send Mary and Johnny to *kindergarten*. . . . Friends will not wave to each other on the street—the raised arm might be taken for a German salute. . . . And while we're about it, let's not forget to discharge professors and school teachers who, in an absent-minded moment, let slip in a good word for German science and culture." [16] As one can see, a deliberate attempt was made in this propaganda to blur the distinction between "anti-Germanism" and "anti-Nazism."

In addition, after America's entry into hostilities, they dealt fatalistically with the concept that Germany was certain to win the war, that German fifth-columnists in America were a menace to the USA war effort, and that resistance to Hitler was national suicide. "In a race where the stakes are so big," stated one speaker, "it is sheer folly to put your money on the wrong horse," [17] referring to our alliance with Great Britain.

The tirades themselves ranged in style from the monologues of peppery Gertie Hahn (who pretended to be a switchboard operator on the *Pittsburgh Tribune* transmitting a scoop to her girl friend "Nancy" on a conspiracy of Jewish publishers) to topical "news" broadcasts with names like "Listen and Learn" and "Topical Talks."

The titles of the broadcasts are revealing in themselves and indicate the range of interest which Dr. Goebbels hoped to arouse in his propaganda in the USA, "Zeesen's Women's Club" was directed to housewives, "The College Hour" to highbrows and "The Economic Review" to business men; "Charley's Cabaret" and "Mr. Okay" were scandal-mongering programs; Constance Drexel used her (genuine) upper-class breeding for a program directed to high society; "Dear Harry" and "The Folks Back Home" were performed by homespun monologists with Midwest accents; "Jim and Johnny" were unemployed workers who aired their gripes; and a series called "The Jew in American History" was a pseudo-literary exposé of "little-known facts" in our heritage.

Some of the programs, particularly the news broadcasts of E. D. Ward and "The College Hour" (which simulated classroom procedure) dealt in eye-witness reports, authoritative tones, and portentous words. Others, notably the scandalslingers and Miss Drexel, pitched their material in a more intimate manner, speaking "confidentially" and in a "homespun" manner. Fred Kaltenbach, an Iowan indicted for treason at the war's end, made the latter approach his specialty, reporting on German matters for the "folks back home," to whom he gave the real "lowdown" on the Nazis.

The star performer in Goebbels' line-up did not broadcast to the United States. He was an Anglophobe by the name of William Joyce,[18] erstwhile author of a pro-Nazi book entitled *Twilight Over England;* Joyce broadcast to Britain as "Lord Haw Haw," satirist of the English upper classes and the aristocrat-Jewish conspiracy which, he claimed, was purposely leading the British Empire to destruction.

There is little doubt that Joyce—or his alter ego Haw Haw—succeeded in getting under the skin of the British and that, of greater importance, he was listened to by thousands of English men and women. It is also certain that, during the darkest days of the Battle of Britain, his acid wit, cocksure announcements of an early German victory, and proclivity for scattering seeds of doubt about the integrity and foresight of the British leaders had some marked effect on British morale.

It is claimed by some that the effects of his broadcasts backfired against Dr. Goebbels and generated an even greater determination in the citizens of Britain to withstand the attacks of the Luftwaffe by working all the harder to give the Germans treatment in kind. Joyce's effectiveness is attested to, however, by the fact that the British did not hesitate to execute him at the war's end, even though his contribution to the Nazi cause had been made up entirely of *words* and he had, essentially, done nothing more than *talk* against his native country.

Joyce's success resulted from his superior knowledge of the British mentality, British humor, and the sore spots in the British make-up. He was actually born in the United States of an Irish father and mother, but the English, who finally sent him to his death, convicted him as a traitor anyway, so intense was the fire he had aroused. Having spent his ten years in Britain, he studied at the University of London, and during his college years came under the influence of Sir Oswald Mosley, whose British Union of Fascists was the English equivalent of our own German-American Bund. Eventually he ended up as Mosley's Propaganda Minister, a sort of British equivalent of Dr. Goebbels—on a much smaller scale.

In 1939, as the noxious vapor of war was precipitating over Europe, Joyce ducked to Germany, and his sardonic creation, Lord Haw Haw, was first heard on short-wave radio in Britain almost immediately after war was declared in September, 1939.

No one who has heard Joyce's phony upper-class accents is likely to forget them. In the early days of the war an estimated 50 per cent of the British public listened to his anti-Semitic, anti-aristocratic appeals to the English to surrender to Germany. But eventually his audience grew tired of him, and it is said that as the tide of war turned away from the German side, even Dr. Goebbels soured on his haughty satire.

The following sample—from a transcript of a privately monitored broadcast by Joyce, probably made shortly after he began his transmissions—will give the reader some of the flavor of his approach:

> There is a line of verse well-known in England that has acquired a terrible significance today. Where are you going, all you big steamers? Where indeed?

To the bottom of the sea, by hundreds of thousands of tons each week.

Down, down they go, with the brave men who man them, because Churchill, unlike the Fuehrer, saw some reason why the war must continue.

When Germany held the European coast from Narvik to Biarritz, when through occupation, or friendly relations, the whole resources of the European continent were open to her, the mountebanks of Downing Street had the cool insolence to tell their long-suffering people they were now about to intensify the blockade against Germany. . . .

Now Germany has had enough of Churchill's nonsense! Since the offer of peace, which the Fuehrer went out of his way to make, has been flatly rejected, the war will be brought to a close expeditiously by the force which the dictator of England prefers since he and his fellow conspirators are irresponsible political frauds who have already secured their future in America and Canada. . . .

How terrible their position is, the British public does not know. It will have seen no warning from its rulers, who do not propose to share the people's fate.

Even yet, the great attack has not begun.

But it is sad beyond words if the people of England *think* that nothing is happening. Their fate is being decided every minute. And yet, they could have decided their own destinies by accepting the Fuehrer's offer of peace. That their own Churchill would condemn them to death and ruin, illustrates the supreme principle of tragedy, which is not disaster by chance, but disaster through opportunity lost.

For words like these, broadcast to England, Mr. Joyce was silenced eventually once and for all. One can understand the degree of wrath such cool needling evoked in Britain—especially since it was couched in the accents of the upper classes.

The broadcasters to the United States boasted no talents so formidable as those of Joyce. A minor league team, however, broadcast regularly to the United States and attempted to achieve what Joyce was apparently doing in Britain.[19]

Basically, the American broadcasters had articulated, probably under Dr. Goebbels' direction, sixteen specific themes which it was thought, would bend American sympathies toward the Nazis. If they display a certain lack of sophistication in regard to the mentality of Americans at the time, two important considerations must be entered to qualify them: first, the broadcasters were operating in a considerable vacuum at a great distance from the United States; second, in relationship to values, morals, ethos, and even sore spots and vulnerabilities, America is a highly heterogeneous nation, neither so tight and territorially unified as Great Britain nor so cohesive in terms of traditions and way of life. Their propaganda objective was, therefore, infinitely more difficult to crystallize than that undertaken by Joyce. Neither do these broadcasters appear to have shared Joyce's extraordinary gadfly talent at persuasion and knowledge of how to exploit his themes.

The radio themes were:

    1. The United States is corrupt, being manipulated by the war-mongering Jewish and Communistic menace.
    2. The foreign policies of the United States are imperialistic and predatory.
    3. President Roosevelt is a tool of Jews, Communists, plutocrats.
    4. The same can be said for Great Britain.
    5. The same can be said for Great Britain's foreign policies.
    6. The same can be said for Winston Churchill.
    7. Nazi Germany is the incarnation of virtue.
    8. So is Japan.
    9. Nazi Germany is strong and will win World War II.
    10. Japan is strong and will also win.
    11. The United States is weak and will lose the war.
    12. The same can be said for Great Britain.

13. The allies are distrustful, deceitful, and envious of one another.

14. The United States and the world are threatened by Communists.

15. Also by Jews.

16. Also by plutocrats.[20]

With a little give-and-take here and there, it is interesting that these same themes are remarkably similar to those currently employed against the United States by Soviet broadcasters from Moscow. See Chapter 3 for further details. Note, moreover, that the long shadow of Goebbels still seems to be upon us, although he would doubtless spin in his grave if he could hear the way Communist Khrushchev's henchmen are still singing, with new words, the songs for which he wrote the music.

The method by which these propagandists worked has been outlined by Hans Fritzsche, a defendant at the Nuremberg War Crimes Trials and official in the Propaganda Ministry, who later cooperated with those who studied the methods of Nazi propaganda.[21] (Fritzsche, incidentally, had gained considerable prominence as a speaker on the German radio solely because of the uncanny similarity of his speaking voice to the cultured tones of Paul Joseph Goebbels!)

Fritzsche claims successes for German short-wave broadcasts to North and South America in the nineteen-thirties. About them, he has stated: ". . . We deal[t] with each scandal, each corruption, each social stress, each strike, each protest against low wages, against long hours of work, or similar things. Not directly, but the moment there was such a strike, the fact was more or less adroitly used to give the corresponding example from Germany, where no strike was in evidence or where the miners received life insurance. We also used a few small tricks. We said to the people of North America, if you have any suggestions for our radio program in your zone, telegraph us *at our expense*. We gathered some interesting statistics. The misuse of this institution never rose to more than 10 per cent." [22]

Fritzsche also explained that, during the war, German broadcasters often made frequent use of those American prisoners of war who, for one reason or another, were not hesitant to provide the Huns with information which could be woven into the broadcasts. Of course, before the war, no such sources of information were available. Reliance was placed upon conventional sources (newspapers, magazines, etc.) and the German businesses and agencies previously discussed, operating quite openly in the United States. Along with consulates and embassies, they provided before World War II the bulk of raw data upon which Dr. Goebbels and assistants like Fritzsche hung the themes we have listed above.

We have been dealing here with German propaganda at some length, not out of any respect for Dr. Goebbels or for his maniacal boss, but rather because, in this introductory survey of the modern arts of persuasion, Nazi propaganda stands as something of a landmark. In the brain of Dr. Goebbels was articulated a concept of subjugation by words more fully conceptualized than by any persuader in history before. The possible exception might be Nikolai Lenin, as we shall see in the next chapter, but Lenin died in 1924 before the technical advances of mass communications had given him instruments to realize his theories. Lenin's concepts had to be implemented by others who lacked his clarity of vision and single-minded purpose.

Goebbels, on the other hand, began his official tour of duty in 1933; the channels of mass communication were fully developed and waiting for him to begin using them for his purposes. He had the full backing of his chief of state and any and all resources required for the subjugation of the will of the German people to the poisonous doctrine of Nazism.

Never before in history had *all* the characteristics of persuasion met so neatly and entirely in one country at one time as in Dr. Paul Joseph Goebbels' Propaganda Ministry from 1933 to 1945. What were the distinctive contributions, then, of Dr. Goebbels to the arts of mass persuasion? They may be summarized as follows:

1. Goebbels, the propagandist, was a genuine fanatic; he believed his doctrine and believed it absolutely.

2. Goebbels was a well-educated man, skilled in literary arts and oratory and possessed of a flair for the colorful, the theatrical, the arresting.

3. Goebbels conceived of propaganda as being *total*—that is, related to every aspect of life, not just to political problems.

4. Every instrument of communication in the Third Reich was used for persuasion.

5. Goebbels saw propaganda as an *instrument of policy*. It was essential that political, military, and economic strategy be formulated with propaganda objectives and results in mind.

6. Conversely, no propaganda was worthwhile which was not geared to political, military, and economic realities. (Toward the end of his career, Dr. Goebbels violated this principle extensively—particularly in reporting to the German people great victories on the Russian front which had been, in fact, the sorriest of defeats. As his diaries indicate, this disregard of his own rules of the game he accomplished with his eyes open, perhaps at the urging of Hitler and others who were desperately worried about morale on the German home front.)

7. Goebbels also knew that the content of propaganda in terms of logic, rationality, and internal consistency of arguments was far less important than the psychological realities of *what his audience needed or wanted to hear*. Therefore, certain arguments which to the observer might seem foolish or self-contradictory were effective propaganda in Germany. It must be remembered that Germany had suffered defeat in World

War I, had lost her proud army, had suffered a crippling infla-
tion in the nineteen-twenties, and was for fifteen or so years the
underdog in the European community of nations.

Are we entitled to say that Dr. Goebbels' propaganda was
successful? Can he be credited with a gold star in our lexicon
of great propagandists in history? Or does the end of the Third
Reich in the spring of 1945, dishonored and defeated, and the
fact that his name has become a symbol of all that is twisted
and diabolical about the regime allow us to call him a failure
and write him off as a nonentity?

The truth lies somewhere between these two extremes, if
we put aside for the moment the natural revulsion one feels
when faced with evaluating men of the stripe of Paul Joseph
Goebbels. On home grounds—and in managing the minds of
his fellow Germans—Dr. Goebbels' record of accomplishment
is not to be scoffed at. By means of his formulas he managed
to convince a civilized, well-educated nation with a long and
impressive history of humanitarian and scientific traditions to
accept a philosophy of barbarism and mysticism which, despite its attempts to exploit various facets of German history,
nevertheless stood for everything antithetical to the best that
could be found in the German heritage. And if, as is presently
claimed, he did not succeed in "selling" this philosophy (or
anti-philosophy) to most Germans, at least he convinced
enough to silence—or reduced to apathy—his critics to insure
the hegemony of the Nazi madness in Germany for a dozen
years right through a humiliating and total defeat in World
War II.

On the other hand, this success also meant Dr. Goebbels'
failure. So intensively did he concentrate his resources on the
Third Reich, so total was his conquest of the German mind
and so absolute was his faith in the perfection of his Fuehrer,
that his very successes at home precluded the kind of vision

that might have permitted him to become a more effective propagandist abroad. First, he lacked—nor could he develop —his "total" propaganda overseas; such persuasion as he bespoke is anathema to the democratic mind and the democratic spirit. Its tone, its irrationality, and its plea for the total submergence of the will and the spirit to its cause challenge the very principles of pluralism and controversy in the free market place of ideas that are germane to the survival of democracy.

Second, such propaganda is difficult to export by its very nature. Dr. Goebbels knew the German mind, but the German mind in the 'twenties, 'thirties, and 'forties was decidedly different from the American mind, the British mind, and the French mind. And here he committed his cardinal sin as a propagandist: he believed that whatever it was that appealed to the German sense of honor and life values would also appeal to others in different cultures who lived in ways unlike German ways and who prized different things in life and held different kinds of aspirations for their respective futures.

This partially explains both Dr. Goebbels' successes and his failures—coupled with the fact that he was on the losing team. It is comforting to remember that men like Dr. Goebbels have frequently pitched their tents in the losing camp and have been vanquished. Up to the present, that is, they have displayed an attraction for defeat and a talent for bringing about their own destruction. It is toward that present that we shall turn now, with an eye to the future. Let us remember, however, that that future may be neither as comforting for us nor as inclined to happy endings as was the past.

THE VOICE OF RED SQUARE

From *the* Soviet Political Dictionary (*1958*):

Propaganda: *The dissemination and elucidation of certain ideas, doctrines, and political theories. Propaganda is of a class and party character. Unlike agitation, propaganda engages in the dissemination of a broader body of ideas and in their more profound and thorough elucidation among a comparatively narrower circle of people.*

Agitation: *A way of political influence over the masses by means of talks, reports, and speeches at meetings, through newspapers, books, brochures, leaflets, the radio and motion pictures et al. Agitation is distinctly on a mass scale and consists in the dissemination among the broad masses of a body of ideas and knowledge narrower in scope and content than in propaganda.*

CHAPTER **3**

WHATEVER it is called, agitation or propaganda, mass persuasion today in the USSR is rooted in the thought of the patron saint founder of the ideal of modern world communism, Nikolai Lenin.

Lenin's ambitions to extend communism to the four corners of the earth, his belief that the philosophy of Marx is a fundamental truth and statement of the human condition, and his view of the Soviet Union as the vanguard of a world revolution are no secret. Neither is the fact that he regarded the arts of persuasion as fundamental devices for achieving this purpose. "The whole task of the Communists is to be able to *convince* backward elements," he once said. "We must convince first and keep force in reserve. At *any* cost, we must *convince* first and not use force until afterwards." [1]

Like the good Leninists that they are, the men who followed Lenin as rulers of the USSR took his injunction seriously. They are now—and have been since the nineteen-twenties—in the "convincing" stage of the world revolution that they regard as some day inevitable, not only on home grounds but in satellite nations, in Korea, Laos, Vietnam, and behind East Berlin's Iron Curtain. To this end they have amassed the largest and most active propaganda apparatus ever known. It is one that dwarfs Dr. Goebbels' Propaganda Ministry of the Third Reich and makes our own efforts at idea invasion seem tiny by comparison.

Conservative estimates indicate that the USSR spends well in excess of *two billion dollars* a year on this "convincing," quite an investment for a nation that undoubtedly could find other uses for the material and manpower involved in its propaganda program.[2] In fact, some experts claim that the USSR spends $2.00 per year for every citizen of the free world —you and me included—on persuasion, as compared with two cents per year per person for the propaganda put out by all the free nations of the world combined![3]

Whether the investment is worth it or not is anybody's guess. Obviously the Soviets think it is because, without bending every effort to spread their doctrines abroad and to subvert uncommitted and hostile nations, they would not be keeping faith with Lenin's ghost.

On the table of organization, the bosses of the propaganda activities of the USSR are members of the Department of Propaganda and Agitation of the Communist Party Central Committee which is directly responsible to the Politburo, another name for the Presidium of the Communist Party, another name for the ruling Soviet oligarchy. As we saw with the Nazis, the Soviet Foreign Office through its legations, embassies, and consulates abroad also operates important agencies of persuasion—and they answer directly to the same kind of bosses, the Politburo.[4]

Agitprop, as the department is known, and the Foreign Office operate a number of propaganda arms, each one responsible for one or another type of persuasion, directed through one or another medium of communication to one or another target audience. All have the same objective: the spreading of Communist doctrine overseas, the "convincing" which will precede world revolution on the Soviet timetable.

Russian propagandists are schooled like priests at one or another propaganda college inside the Soviet Union.[5] Not all of them are Soviet citizens; many are nationals of other nations (probably including the United States of America) who are inundated with Leninist ideology and Soviet propaganda methods and subsequently turned loose around the world to plead the cause of Khrushchev and Company.

They are taught basically that good Communist propaganda isolates the "weak spot" in the target nation where they are directed to center their activities. Is religious conflict a prime problem, as it is in certain Eastern nations? Is it a weak central government? Failing natural resources? Economic dissension? Race problems? Whatever it is, the Communist propagandist is then instructed in the best methods for harping on the sore spot in order to be able, eventually, to offer communism and the Soviet Union as nostrums for the ailment.

This is the simple key to Soviet propaganda—not the arcane doctrines of Leninism or Marx, but rather the bold and realistic recognition that *if internal dissatisfaction and strife can be stimulated, Communism will look attractive beside it,* even if it is only defined in crude Utopian or idealistic terms. Accordingly, the Soviet propagandist is taught that his persuasion or agitation *need not make sense* in terms of pure Communist theory. That is, he may violate as often and as deeply as necessary the tenets of Marxism-Leninism to achieve his eventual objectives, which are conquest by the Marxist-Leninist way of life.

On a world-wide scale the Soviet line of "coexistence" is an excellent example of this contradiction. On the one hand, the idea of coexistence is absolutely antithetical to pure Communist theory: realizing the correct and inevitable economic and social outcome of history, the Communist theorist *knows* (in his warped view of the world) that capitalism and communism cannot coexist, that Western democracy must inevitably give way to communism. On the other hand, as a well-trained propagandist, he is ready to *pretend* that coexistence is a genuine possibility and that he is anxious to achieve it, if he believes that his pretense will facilitate his objective—the end of coexistence and Communist conquest of the world.

This is the cold-blooded basic training the Soviet Union gives her persuaders, training actually in intellectual espionage, because propaganda when conducted in this manner is more like cloak-and-dagger derring-do than mere argumentation or an attempt to convince an uncommitted public of an ideology. In this way, propaganda from Red Square is even more insidious than Hitler's foul persuasion; in international persuasion at least, the Third Reich's spokesmen were hesitant to contradict their own ideologies to win converts. Soviet propagandists have no such scruples, and this is one reason why the Western mind is so frequently baffled at the inconsistencies and shifts in the words which come to us from Moscow.

International radio propaganda in the Soviet Union is handled directly by the Foreign Office. Here, in the Administration of the Central Broadcasting or Foreign Broadcasting Sector, various units are in charge of overseas broadcasting, each in a different language—about 40 or so in all. Because this agency is so closely related to the Foreign Office (the equivalent of our State Department) and the Presidium, it can keep close tabs on the current party lines, policies, and objectives of the government, just as the bosses in the Politburo can keep a vigilant eye on their propagandists who are feeding the Russian view of history to the world.

The International Book Publishing Corporation, which is an arm of Russia's Ministry of Trade, distributes books in many languages throughout the world, as does the Foreign Section of the State Literary Publishers. Also distributed widely are a number of periodicals published in Russian, Korean, English, Chinese, German, French, and Spanish, some of which find their way to the United States. SOV Informburo, Tass, and SOVfoto (part of Tass) are news agencies which disseminate Communist propaganda to Communist line publications abroad and to other journals eager for news about the Soviet Union. Most of the material they supply is, of course, persuasion in the interests of the Soviet Union. SOVfilm Movie Distributing Agency does likewise with films, sending them to countries where they are likely to get distribution.

But conventional media for the distribution of Russian propaganda are by no means the only way the USSR exports its ideas to the free world and its satellites. The All-Union Society for Cultural Relations with Foreign Countries—known as VOKS—is also in the business, along with the state travel bureau Intourist, of arranging cultural exchanges and receiving and sending delegations from and to other countries. These travelers from the USSR have almost always been indoctrinated in the best formal and informal propaganda techniques for handling the nationals they are likely to meet on their visits. In addition to cultural exchanges, VOKS handles the distribution of various kinds of pro-Soviet literature overseas.

Apart from all these avenues of propaganda, the USSR makes use of Red-front organizations like the World Peace Council abroad and the Partisans of Peace and American

Peace Crusade here in the United States to spread the party line wherever and whenever possible. Also, Russia's relatively secret underground international revolutionary network, the much feared Cominform (once known as the Comintern), mixes together espionage, subversion, and Red propaganda to blanket the world with words and ideas from Red Square.

The Soviets, of course, give special attention to those publics in whom they see the greatest potentialities for giving a boost to the spread of world communism. Most notable among these are anti-Communist exiles from the captive nations whom Soviet propaganda attempts in various ways to lure back to their respective homelands.[6] An agency, located in East Berlin and called the Committee for Return to Home, is the source of quantities of documents in various languages of the captive nations with names like "Voice of the Fatherland" and "Fatherland," exhorting exiles to return home and submit to the Communist domination of their native countries. Naturally, most Soviet embassies and consulates have "attachés" who work in the free nations of the world to encourage (by words or sometimes by force or fear of reprisals against families or friends) exiles from these countries to come back to the countries of their birth and to work for the Reds who are presently running it.

All of this indicates a massive network of outlets for Communist propaganda, a good share of it directed to the free world in general and to the United States in particular. Suffice it to say, America has no such comparable or elaborate structure for the spread of her doctrines abroad. We were late and reluctant entrants for the battle of the minds of men and our efforts at overseas persuasion are many times less complex—and many believe less effective—than those of the USSR, which has taken Lenin's initial injunctions about the spread of world communism so literally and has implemented his ideas so wholeheartedly.

Exactly what are the kinds of persuasion which the Kremlin directs against other nations, and, most important, how effective have they been or are they likely to be in the future? [7]

The party line naturally varies from country to country. For nations like Yugoslavia it emphasizes the dangers of alliance with the USA and the might of the Soviet war machine. The same theme is used for Greece. To India the Russians promise peace, independence, and aid. For Indonesia they bear down hard on American "imperialism" and "colonialism." The decadence of American life is the theme they emphasize to Australians and New Zealanders, and for South Africa our friendship with emerging black nations receives special attention. So it varies from country to country—carefully tailored persuasion which realistically evaluates the particular vulnerabilities of the listeners who are likely to hear or see it.

We see here, of course, the *degree* to which Soviet propaganda is spread around the world. A clear idea can also be given by examining the schedule of short-wave broadcasts emanating from Moscow in the course of one week. About 263 hours altogether are directed to Western Europe, about 58 hours to East Europe, and 30 to Yugoslavia in three languages. To the Near East, South Asia, and Africa, Soviet propagandists are on the air 293 hours (broadcasting in thirteen languages); 119 hours to the Far East (in ten languages); 49 hours to Latin America; and 105 hours to North America (in English, Ukrainian, and Yiddish). Along with half a dozen other miscellaneous targets, the grand total of these broadcasts comes to 875 hours of intensive persuasion *by radio alone!* [8]

Certain over-all themes characterize Soviet persuasion of every kind, developed in one way or another according to the psychological mind-set of the victim audience. Suzanne Labin, an expert on Soviet propaganda, whose research in mass persuasion has been published by the United States Congress, has characterized them as follows:[9]

1. The conflict between "two blocs," the USSR and the USA, is complete and absolute. One is either on one side of the fence or on the other.
2. When the USSR commits aggressive acts or takes a warlike stance, it is because she is afraid of the USA.
3. Western nations shut themselves up in a negative attitude.
4. The major problem of the world today is the problem of atomic energy.
5. The many millions of devoted, enthusiastic Communists in the world today are evidence of the success of communism.
6. Communism succeeds because it rights social wrongs, injustices, and evils.
7. Communism and Russia offer the most tangible aid today to the underdeveloped nations.
8. The Soviet Union stands for peace; the Western nations want war.

At the time this book was being written, the major tone of Soviet propaganda was being dictated by the artfulness and clever style of Premier Khrushchev's public personality. While it harps hard on the decadence of Western capitalism and the presence in the free nations of the seeds of their own destruction, it takes the outward aspect that Khrushchev himself shows the world: joviality, subtlety, cleverness, and even a twinge of regret that so great an edifice as Western capitalist civilization must eventually fall before the historical necessity of world communism. "Coexistence and confidence" were Khrushchev's two major themes in his speeches to party bigshots in 1961, and they remain the pivot on which Soviet propaganda policy rests—and probably will rest for a long time to come.

To develop its themes, Soviet propaganda has employed a number of sympathetic listeners with a barrage of arguments, creating confusion, repeating absurd claims, timing their appeals to significant events—such as the second Geneva conference, the moon rocket, or the U-2 incident—and evoking suspense through the Powers trial, the flights of Russian astronauts, demagogy, outright misstatements, lies in terms of accusations against Western nations, and so forth. Some charges are as far-fetched as the "germ warfare" nonsense during the Korean war, but which a goodly number of the earth's citizens probably still believe to this day.[10]

Soviet propaganda is blunt, direct, frequently ingenious, but unsubtle. It is compounded of falsehoods. It is presented in a sledge-hammer manner. It is not easy to understand why and how it is believed by many millions. Like Hitler's persuasion, it frequently depends upon the "big lie." And yet it has been effective—and is effective. It passes the pragmatic test; it works. Let us take a case study to see exactly why.

Some years ago certain Soviet propaganda adopted a line that American interests were out to undermine the Western nations in the interests of the Wall Street, imperialist, decadent capitalists. Not a new theme by any means, the Soviet propagandists managed to put it into a new bottle, a Coca-Cola bottle, to be exact. The way in which Americans were accomplishing this subversion, Soviet propagandists maintained, was by means of the introduction of a noxious American fluid to Western Europe: namely, something called Coca-Cola, fundamentally a vile poison, contributive to impotence in men, sterility in women, falling hair and fallen arches, the pip, the grippe, ague, aches in general, and what have you.

An absurd propaganda line? Sheer nonsense, calculated for propaganda failure? Hogwash, testable with easy reference to the facts that American health seems unaffected by Coca-

Cola consumption and that the simplest chemical analysis can reveal how benign the fizzy fluid really is?

The answer to these questions is an emphatic "yes," *if we are ignorant of the mind-set of the people to whom the message was directed*—which the Soviet propagandist never is. Study the mind of the perceiver and this message which can hardly be dignified by calling it a lie can become a brilliant propaganda coup, the effects of which are probably still being felt to this day in Europe.

This message was directed by the Soviets to the *wine-growers of France*. At the time, they had had a particularly poor year and their economic welfare was far from certain. While they had vast stocks of wine on hand, it was a vintage of poor quality, difficult to sell. In addition, the man who was then Premier of France, Mendes-France, alarmed at the abnormally high rate of alcoholism in his country, had begun a campaign to get Frenchmen to drink more *milk,* a fluid traditionally considered in those climes useful for making cheese and inevitable in breast-feeding—but, in sophisticated opinion, hardly fit for consumption by anyone over the age of three.

Now, what does the French wine-grower think, alarmed about his future, the future of wine-drinking in his country, his own economic status, and other matters? The damned Americans have come along with a displacement for the balm of Bacchus: *Coca-Cola,* a drink which has proved eminently successful wherever it has been introduced, and which is cheaper and safer to swill than wine. *Of course,* says the wine-grower, it is poisonous; *of course,* it rots the teeth, addles brains, causes the shakes, or what have you. *Of course,* the Americans are fiends, degenerates, imperialists, and the like. And more important, says Pierre, in the next election, I'll vote for the Communist candidate!

Foolish falsehood or brilliant persuasion from Red Square? Brilliant persuasion, of course; ruthless, immoral, and cruel, to be sure, but nonetheless realistic and intelligent, carefully thought through, hitting its target with enviable efficiency.

It is not the only example of Soviet trickery and cleverness in using ideas on behalf of the interests of Russia. The aforementioned germ warfare theme of the Korean War is another instance. From the point of view of many neutrals, like the United States, which had not scrupled to use an atomic weapon twice against Japan, would certainly not hesitate to implement its warfare in Korea with bacteriological weapons. The lie seemed reasonable, and almost inevitably helped to damage the image of the United States.

Khrushchev's use of the U-2 plane shot down over the Soviet Union and pilot Powers' confession of spying is still another example. After seeing one of our spies shot down, the conclusion that the United States is an aggressor nation seems highly rational to many people who are concerned about world peace, particularly when they are asked to trust American professions of pacifism.

This is one kind of propaganda which comes from Red Square. The specific media for this persuasion are numerous, and encompass just about every means of communication that men have devised. The propaganda directed specifically against the USA is abundant and devious. Nevertheless, since we are a relatively open society, we have done very little to keep it away from our shores, aside from requiring registration (when materials are printed abroad) of publications of foreign governments and requesting our customs officials to refuse entry to openly subversive materials.

What actually are the media the Soviets use to disseminate their propaganda to us?

First, anyone with a short-wave radio can hear Radio Moscow almost every night of the week. Little is known about the men and women who broadcast to us but, unlike Dr. Goebbels' broadcasters, they are not (or probably not) turn-coat Americans. In a broadcast monitored by the authors, the broadcasters claimed to have been trained in English in the Soviet Union, a claim difficult to believe, considering their Midwest, Southern, or Eastern accents and the excellence of their speech—but possible nevertheless.

They offer news reports, panel discussions, interpretations of the day's news, and talks about life in the Soviet Union. They have even taken to imitating the standard news broadcasting format of American commercial radio, *viz.*, "Those are the headlines; now for the news!" Occasionally, they answer questions supposedly sent them by listeners in the United States. All in all, their broadcasting is lively, interesting, and relaxed, and compares quite favorably in quality with broadcasts by our own "Voice of America." The content is pure party line.

The Soviet Union also distributes in the USA a slick, *Life*-like magazine called *USSR*, edited in Moscow and intended for Americans. About 50,000 copies per issue are circulated. In its early days, the magazine was ponderous, serious, and didactic. Lately, Soviet propagandists seem to have profited from the study of our own international magazine, *Amerika*, which is distributed in the Soviet Union. Today *USSR* is a lively, well-written, and interesting publication.

Soviet propaganda further reaches America via the newspaper *The Worker,* published weekly in the United States by the American Communist Party, and also seeps in through the so-called "National Council of Soviet-American Friendship." While its periodical publications such as *American-Soviet*

Facts and *Culture and Life* are written and edited in the United States, they might as well be sent directly from Red Square, so closely do they follow the propaganda directives from Russia. And, as we have noted, Red propaganda also arrives in the USA via other friendship organizations, youth groups, embassy press releases, news agencies which pick up Tass dispatches, American Communist pressure on labor unions, women's groups, and religious organizations. While Communist influence in these groups is probably less extensive than the John Birchers would have us believe, there is little doubt that certain "ban the bomb" campaigns and peace crusaders get Moscow's blessing and help and, unfortunately, exploit the decent impulses of many individuals who would not join them if they were aware of the Communist aegis.

What are the results of the Soviet investment? Is Khrushchev's two billion dollars per year well spent, or would it better be diverted, from his point of view, to another dam on the Dnieper? Is it bringing about the worldwide swing to Communism that Lenin had predicted? These questions are difficult to answer finally; it is doubtful if even Mr. Khrushchev could respond to them with too much certainty.

One significant advantage that Khrushchev's propaganda chiefs have over the free nations is the unity and uniformity of the Soviet state. A closed society can respond quickly and efficiently to events—can modulate its propaganda line for short-term strategic goals. Open societies, on the other hand, encourage varying viewpoints on current issues. They have difficulty in effectively transmitting persuasion abroad because of their diversity of ideas and because their propagandists tend to dodge and parry less artfully than their counterparts in monolithic states. However neat the effectiveness of Russian persuasion abroad, this is probably an explanation, in part, of its successes. Explanations are cold comfort, nevertheless, when one examines the scope and reach of the Communist propaganda effort.

In the non-committed nations of the world, it has been claimed that definite sympathy for the Soviet Union has been the result of Soviet persuasion. Coupled with other facts like Soviet technical and economic aid to underdeveloped nations, this is probably true, if we can judge by the leftist leanings of many of the so-called "neutral nations." If it has done nothing else, this Soviet-inspired propaganda has helped to create to a degree a climate of hostility toward the United States which may pay off eventually.

For nations friendly to us, Soviet propaganda has loaded bullets into the guns of the Communist minorities. However, most Frenchmen, Italians and Englishmen, for example, recognize the degree of their self-interest served by close friendship with the USA in political, economic, and military matters. It is a fundamental tenet of persuasion that words or ideas *can never militate against what one regards as his self-interest*. (This, of course, presupposes that one is well aware of where his self-interest lies.) Self interest, in nations which are friendly to us, dictates that the voice from Red Square not be taken too seriously.

As far as Communist propaganda to the United States is concerned, Soviet influence has probably been overstated by those concerned with the fight against communism. The reason that we seem resistant to the appeal of the Communist idea invader and his black art is, of course, obvious: our capitalist economy seems to *work,* our economy is expanding, our bellies are filled; we are fat. Self-interest, again, is a good defense against the voice from Red Square.

Should our economy take a turn for the worse, however, should our race problems, social problems, and lowering of national morale create unrest, confusion, and discontent, then our resistance to the voice from Moscow will inevitably be lowered. Any or all of these eventualities will permit Mr. Khrushchev to point with justice to the failure of capitalism, the decadence of democracy, and the impracticality of Western thought. He will point to our sore spots, and bitter, disillusioned men will listen. Make no mistake! The antidote for the voice from Red Square is the health of the American economy and the élan of the American spirit. We had better take precious care to maintain both.

PART TWO

THE FACE OF AMERICA

WE WERE NEVER LOVELIER

To the European mind, with all its good will, the things that make Americans more powerful make them also more boorish, the things that make them more like giants make them all less like men.

—MAX LERNER [1]

Prior to these meetings [Khrushchev's American trip] many Americans had known less about our country than about the moon. For a long time they had been intimidated by silly tales about the "horrors" of communism. Here before them at last was a live and dynamic, unpretentious and plain-speaking representative of the new world, a man persistent in marking for his goal and capable of standing up for himself.

—*USSR* Magazine [2]

CHAPTER **4**

IN LARGE measure, countries will be judged by both their friends and their enemies by what they are.

This is particularly true of the United States because the USA is an open society, that is, a nation where a minimum of restraints is placed on the flow of information from its shores, and ready access is available for the spread of news within its borders.

For this reason it is important in fighting the cold propaganda war that the image of America we project overseas be as accurate, as full, and even as flattering as it possibly can be. This has not always been the case, and the Red propagandists have frequently made much of our weaknesses without counterbalancing their stories with our strengths. Communist persuaders have crowed consistently about our shortcomings: Little Rock, Arkansas; Oxford, Mississippi; what poverty remains in our affluent society; and other sore spots on the body of our culture.

This propaganda advantage for the Reds is probably one of the prices we have to pay for our open society, and, as we shall see, a price which is likely to be worth paying. There are occasions, however, when we apparently go out of our way to offer the world a picture of the United States which makes us look immature, infantile, and stupid. This has happened all too frequently in recent years, and in each instance the incident or occasion which caused the poor propaganda could have been prevented. In each instance it was a clever Red idea invader who took advantage of some foolish move on our part which unnecessarily exposed to the world one vulnerable aspect of American life.

Take the case of Nikita S. Khrushchev, for instance.

Whatever else he is, Khrushchev is no fool, though he sometimes deliberately acts like one. This is nothing more than play-acting, however, on the part of a peculiarly protean character.

"He looks like a devil," a New York taxi driver offered us gratuitously. "When I seen him on that balcony of the Legation on Sixty-eighth Street—I was as near to him as I am to that dame with the poodle on the sidewalk—you couldn't miss that little pig face. And them eyes!"

Khrushchev has been compared in the press and elsewhere to Foxy Grandpa, a cherub, a petulant baby, a character actor, and other less complimentary things. His portrait on the cover of *Time* magazine, during a period when the cold war raged, undoubtedly looked diabolical. At the time of the thaw, a subsequent likeness in the same magazine took on kindly characteristics—even joviality.

One thing is certain: he is a master of the art of persuasion. Like all good propagandists, he is both tough and smart. When one thinks of the kind of people—men like Molotov, Beria, Malenkov—on whose backs Khrushchev climbed to the top of the Russian power pyramid, one may well shudder. Political advancement in the United States is but child's play contrasted with power politics in the Soviet Union. Common sense says that the man who seizes leadership in that witches' cauldron must be as hard as a diamond coated with tungsten.

The raw facts of Mr. K's background check with this assumption all the way down the line. He worked his way up from nowhere with his muscles and his brain. Born in poverty, he labored in coal mines, tended sheep, and slaved at menial jobs. He was beaten, kicked, and whipped, and before he had learned to read, he had learned to fight and scheme. After the Russian Revolution, he fought his way upward through Soviet bureaucracies in the Donets Basin, the Ukraine, and Moscow. And wherever he was and whatever he did, he came out on top.

Khrushchev knows his Marx—but he knows his men, too. His views of capitalism, of the United States, of Christianity, of democracy, or even of history may be distorted, but they are sharp and realistic in terms of what is or is not good propaganda for the Soviet Union. Before he acts—be it to pound a shoe on a table at the United Nations, drink a vodka toast with a foreign correspondent, or buss an astronaut—it is a sure bet that he has calculated the consequence of what he does and the effect it will have on the minds of the people in his own country and abroad.

It requires no expertise in diplomacy not to trust him an inch and to make sure—when you play poker with him in the open forum and the chips are propaganda victories—that all your errors are on the side of conservatism and caution. Yet the history of America's attitude toward Nikita Khrushchev is one of startling naïveté.

Remember the time—it was not so long ago—when Khrushchev was touring the Iron Curtain circuit with Marshal Bulganin? Mr. K was making his final thrust for the dictatorship of the Soviet Union. Stalin had died in 1953; his throne was occupied by Malenkov until 1955. Then Malenkov was kicked out in favor of Khrushchev and exiled to do a tour of duty as Minister of Electric Power Stations in a cool climate. In those days, mindless of the facts that were staring us in the face, our journalists pegged Khrushchev exactly as he wanted his image to be construed (clearly to his advantage, as subsequent events have shown). Back then we persisted in calling Bulganin and Khrushchev "B" and "K," and our press wizards treated them as if they were a pair of buffoons.

Later events—in Geneva, Moscow, and, ironically, on Park Avenue, USA—have revealed the true picture. The Soviet Union is being run by skillful administrators and politicians, ruthlessly opposed to the Western democracies—to the very spirit, if not the letter, of democracy and freedom. Khrushchev, in his own words, is out to "bury us" politically and economically.

"B" and "K" indeed! Looking backward, it is just this phrase and everything it connotes, including the simpleminded estimate by our "experts" of the nature of our enemies, that provided the setting for a strange incident to be described presently.

To understand this incident and to abstract its truth or its meaning for the propagandist, it is necessary for a moment to consider first Nikita Khrushchev's moral code in regard to—of all things—sex.

Like all of us, Khrushchev developed his morals probably almost entirely as a reflection of the society in which he has grown up. The key to understanding them—and their relationship to the story which follows—requires a brief look at evidence available to all, laymen and experts alike, at almost any public library in the United States, evidence about the role of sex in Soviet life.[3]

Even granting the cultural diversity of the peoples of the USSR, most Russians, in terms of our reference, are decidedly conservative and prudish in their moral viewpoints, especially when it comes to sex. It is true that Friedrich Engels, one of the fathers of communism was not, but he was a German living in England (and a tired business man as well), not a Russian. Engels had campaigned in the late nineteenth century for the emancipation of women from the home, the destruction of the conventional family, and the abolition of the concept of illegitimacy of children, all of which would provide social sanctions for a pretty frisky sort of moral code.

Because of what Engels had written, the Russians did attempt, after the 1917 revolution, to put these ideas into action. In 1919 Madame Alexandra Kollontai had begun a "free love" movement, much publicized and little understood abroad, with legalized abortions, post-card divorces, and unregistered marriages. By the end of the 1930's the wind had gone out of the sails; the movement was abandoned for the most part, and the Russians went back to their strait-laced ways.

The reforms left some mark on Soviet culture. Women had, indeed, been emancipated—from the home to the factory, streetcar, and battlefield. But in matters of sex, the Russians had bounced back to traditional standards: a morality essentially middle class, puritanical, and conservative by our standards. Their rules of decorum and proper respectable attitudes, both private and public, in matters of fidelity, pre- and extra-marital sex relations, and obscene behavior are rigid and uncompromising, what we in America call "Victorian."

The odds are high that this kind of decorum and these morals are also Nikita Khrushchev's. And Khrushchev's morals and sense of propriety were his secret weapons in the propaganda advantage he gained on the United States during the events of the afternoon of September 19, 1959, a day which, to paraphrase Roosevelt, is likely to "live in idiocy."

Nikita Khrushchev and his entourage had arrived in the United States four days before on what was hoped here would be a good-will mission, but which might have been anticipated (and was, by some) as just another skirmish in the cold propaganda war.

Mr. K's gigantic TU-104 had deposited him at Andrews Air Force Base in Maryland, where he was greeted by President Eisenhower and what the charitable would call a "mixed reaction" from the American people who, it seems, did not know quite what to make of the little man who emerged from the big airplane. While many Americans obeyed President Eisenhower's request to treat the visitor with courtesy, Khrushchev saw two types of American hostility leveled at him. He reacted to them both with cleverly varied petulance, belligerence, and humor—which made us look relatively silly and petty.

First, there was the relatively orderly opposition of those who, in one way or another, represented interests in the Iron Curtain countries. These interests looked forward to eventual liberation from Soviet tyranny and believed that agitation would further their cause. Placards, signs, posters, and the stony faces of pickets met Khrushchev continually during his trip—especially in New York City. All in all, the effect of these protests did no harm when reflected in the mirror of world opinion; they demonstrated tangibly (and with some restraint) the process of free expression in the United States and served also to remind others of the imperialistic behavior of the USSR in recent years.

On the other hand, Khrushchev was also greeted with a kind of boorish aggressiveness that must have come as quite a shock to him at first. It manifested itself in a loud, self-assured voice which rang to the rafters with the conviction that "we" (whoever the "we's" of the moment happened to be) were the most perfect specimens in all of recorded history; this was the moment of our absolute glory and everyone opposed to us must be bad, depraved, foul, sinful, ignorant, and treacherous.

The sum total of the reaction—friendly and hostile—was ambiguous enough for the foreign press to make what it would of it for its own purposes. Naturally, it differed in different nations, depending on whether sentiment was with us, against us, or neutral. The Soviet line used our hostility in this way: "In his speech at the meeting in Moscow on his return," a Soviet magazine reported, "Khrushchev told the truth about his stay in this complex and contradictory country; about the cordiality with which he was received by the people and the anger betrayed by certain persons hostile to us. Someone evidently counted on provoking Khrushchev, and somehow baiting and upsetting him, and thus diverting the whole undertaking onto the bumpy road of the 'cold war.' But after the failure of such attempts, American newspapers began to carry respectful headlines about the 'man of iron,' as they now referred to Nikita S. Khrushchev." [4]

Opportunities like this for overt distortion by the Red press would, of course, have been curtailed had Mr. K been met by American people informed by their leaders of the propaganda realities of the visit: namely, that *they* as well as their visitors were on trial in the court of world opinion, and that Khrushchev had every intention of using *them* as bullets in his propaganda machine gun. It was no surprise, however, to hear that the sky-written white cross with which some religious zealot had thought to decorate the heavens above New York City upon Nikita's arrival had been reported by the Soviet press as a giant "K"! Thus the taste displayed by the sky-writer was so radically (or intentionally) misunderstood by Communist observers as to be distorted easily into an affirmative symbol for Mr. Khrushchev.

And the press, both American and foreign, ran riot, displaying even more consistent irresponsibility than the worst of our common men. With a kind of boorishness that seems universally to distinguish some journalists on the job, they cooed and chuckled with mannerless avidity over Nikita during his thirteen days in the United States. Some of them were injured in the line of duty: pelleted with corn by Iowa farmer Roswell Garst at his farm at Coon Rapids; kicked, shoved, or pushed while snooping.

The journalists were out in full force. Over 300 newsmen representing the fourth estate of seventeen countries tagged along on K's tour with their cameras, teletypes, microphones, and gimmickry of mass communications. American TV networks alone probably spent over two million dollars on the trip, and one network estimates that 375 of its cameramen and technicians covered the festivities.

Of course the irony of the press rhubarb was that, annoyed as Khrushchev may have appeared, the antics of the scribes provided a secret weapon for his psychological warfare. Harry Schwartz of the *New York Times* has pointed out that our State Department obliged the Premier by deciding "at the last moment to let all those who wanted to cover the visit do so." [5] Many wanted to, and, probably to Khrushchev's delight, they behaved like hooligans at the same time that they publicized to a news-hungry public around the world the manipulations of the most adroit spokesman for Soviet Communism in the world today.

The eye of the hurricane, Premier K himself, arrived in Los Angeles, California, at exactly 12:10 P.M., September 19, 1959, Hollywood time, after a transcontinental flight of five hours and twenty-seven minutes. The weather was magnificent. The previous four days had been busy ones, filled with press conferences, meetings, and dinners along with a little

sight-seeing. But make no mistake. Nikita was here in the
United States neither to look nor to listen. He had come to *talk*
—ostensibly to American citizens and statesmen, but mostly
to potentially receptive ears thousands of miles away both inside and outside of the Iron Curtain. He had seen diplomats,
newsmen, civic officials, business men, and economists. Now
he was being steered to the near-mythical city of Hollywood
with its unique cast of characters.

Who decided to show Hollywood to the old master? The
chances are that we shall never know, but in its way it was an
appropriate choice. Nikita could not have done better himself.
Hasn't the image of America in the minds' eyes of millions of
people abroad been the direct result of Hollywood's extensive
exportation of its celluloid amusements? Wasn't it entirely fit-
ting that this image, for what it is worth, be ironically manipulated now by the one man best able to ram it down our
throats?

No sooner had his plane touched the ground, than he was
whisked by limousine to the Twentieth Century-Fox Film studios for a fancy luncheon.[6] As one Hollywood wag observed
the next day, "Twentieth Century-Fox meets twentieth-
century fox!"

At the studio the tone for the entire afternoon was set almost immediately by Spyros Skouras, head of the movie company, who seemed to spare no opportunity for sniping at the
Soviet Premier.

Apparently provoked by the impolitic and arrogant needling of Skouras, Khrushchev boiled. He must have decided
then and there (in front of an elaborate company of just about
every luminary, every Pepsodent smile, and every low-cut bod-
ice Hollywood could muster) to turn the screws on Hollywood.

Here is a sample of the repartee with Skouras:

SKOURAS: How many Prime Ministers are there in Russia?
KHRUSHCHEV: How many Presidents are there in the United
States? . . .
SKOURAS: We have 2,000 American presidents of American
corporations!

(Khrushchev, red-faced, explained rather cogently to his
host at this point how power in the USSR is distributed.)

KHRUSHCHEV: There, Comrade Greek, is that not enough for
you?
SKOURAS: No, that's a monopoly!
KHRUSHCHEV: It is a *people's* monopoly. . . . [A leader in the
Soviet Union] does not possess anything but the pants he
wears. It all belongs to the *people*. . . .
SKOURAS: No—*you* know the president; he works for you!

The badgering got so bad at this point that, as *Time* magazine reports, the assembled guests had the temerity to shout
to Skouras, "Shut up," "Sit down," and "Let him alone"—
words for which, under ordinary circumstances, some of them
would have been exiled to the insecurities of Central Casting.[7]
    The fat was in the fire, though, and Mr. K, whatever else
he had intended to do that afternoon, let loose. He crowed
about the Soviet economy and Soviet life. Then, with deadly
acumen, he let the "distinguished company" of Hollywood
performers—symbols, among the intelligentsia of the world,
of the vacuity of the movies they had made for years—have it
with a straight face:
    "We in the Soviet Union love and esteem the intellectuals,
the people of intellectual toil. And *you* represent not just intellectual toil but what is the *finest* in that. You represent the
arts! And you require the gentlest of treatment, the best treatment as an orchid which requires humidity and warmth and
light. . . .
    "Now I have a question for you. What country has the best

ballet? Yours? You do not even have a permanent opera and
ballet theater. . . . Our theatrical arts—I am not going to
lavish my praise on them. But say to yourselves, which art is
on the downgrade? *Our* cinema art? *Yours!*"

It was almost as if the old man knew exactly what had
been prepared for him by the movie colony. He went on to
talk about serious Soviet films and the contribution to them by
Mikhail Sholokov, author of "The Fate of Man," "Quiet Flows
the Don," and "Virgin Soil Upturned," who was present.

Then came the outburst that subsequently made the big
headlines, but probably served Khrushchev's propaganda purposes less efficiently than later events that day. The outburst,
however, provided some comic relief for the Premier and indicated that this particular part of his trip was being managed
by home-grown incompetents.

His tour of Disneyland was cancelled because Police Chief
William H. Parker of the Los Angeles Police Department
claimed that he could not offer Mr. K adequate protection!
The rest is history.

"But just now I was told that I could not go to Disneyland," stormed Khrushchev. "I asked, 'Why not? What is it—
do you have rocket launching pads there?' I do not know. And
just listen—just listen to what I was told—what reason I was
told. We, which means *American authority, cannot guarantee
your security.*

"What is it? Is there an epidemic of cholera there or something? Or have gangsters taken hold of the place who can destroy me? . . . I cannot find words to explain this to my people.

"Come to *our* country. I will personally accompany anyone any place and no foreign guest will see anything but respect." [8]

Khrushchev never saw Disneyland—but he saw something a good deal more useful for his purposes than Mickey Mouse.

If Nikita himself had written the script, it couldn't have rolled more perfectly! Everything that had happened up to now was preamble. The Premier of the USSR was about to see American culture in its fullest flower: he was off to watch the *shooting of a movie*. This brings us to the incident alluded to earlier, and here is where sex and morality enter the story.

Undoubtedly the Hollywood reception committee had Mr. K sized up: they took him for a bald-headed old codger, a sucker for a peek at female thighs, bosoms, well-rounded buttocks. Knowing nothing about life or morality in the USSR, and committing the great American sin of believing that our weaknesses and strengths are everybody's weaknesses and strengths, the committee could hardly be expected to arrive at a realistic judgment.

Having finished their luncheon, Khrushchev and his party were ushered onto a sound stage of the studio where, in the words of the *New York Times*' Murray Schumach,[9] had been erected "a sort of private box" for the visiting Russians. From this private box, the guests were greeted by Frank Sinatra, who then introduced Louis Jourdan and Maurice Chevalier, co-stars with him in the film "Can-Can," the shooting of which the Premier was shortly to inspect.

Jourdan and Chevalier did a number called "Live and Let Live," and Sinatra naturally could not resist the temptation to abstract a moral from the title. "I think it's a marvelous idea," quipped Frankie, which must have pleased Nikita no end. The Premier grinned.

Sinatra now explained the plot of the mighty opus Khrushchev was to watch. "It's a movie about a lot of pretty girls and the fellows who like pretty girls," he explained in his best tutorial manner. "Later in the movie," he went on, "we go

into a saloon. A saloon is a place where you go to drink."
Khrushchev laughed. Sinatra sang "C'est Magnifique," a song
from the film. It was all very nice.

Then came the girls!

First, Shirley MacLaine, dressed in a hopped-up Holly-
woodian version of France's answer to Victorianism, mumbled
a few banalities in Russian. Then, along with Juliet Prowse,
Miss MacLaine joined a bevy of comely chorines in a red-
blooded, all-American, authentic French can-can dance. The
girls, in the words of Mr. Schumach, "pranced on stage, with
shrill cries, kicking their legs and whirling in the traditional
patterns of the can-can." [10] This means, simply, that plenty of
backsides, thighs, and garters were visible, and since Mr.
Khrushchev's private box was elevated above the sound stage
itself, the Premier unquestionably had an opportunity for interesting camera angles of the cuties.

Whether Khrushchev was, in fact, *shocked* is irrelevant.
He probably was, in the light of what we have seen about Russian morality, but it matters little. When the dance was com-
pleted, he was, all in all, quite polite, commenting merely that
the dance suited the picture—an incontestably apt critical
opinion—and that he was no expert on night clubs.

In any event, it seemed to take a little time for the import
of the events of the afternoon to sink into the wily Premier's
psyche and activate his propaganda glands. The press was
chortling about the Disneyland episode, while Khrushchev di-
gested his cultural experience on the Fox lot. It did not take
long.

That evening, at a dinner in his honor in Los Angeles, he
couldn't resist a quick jab, and the direction of his thinking
came clear to the public in an awful moment of discovery.

Said Khrushchev, "Los Angeles is the center of the American motion picture industry. It exerts a tremendous influence

on the life of the society. . . . It is therefore important for the motion picture people to decide which purpose this mighty art will serve [a leaf, incidentally, from Lenin's book]. In our country, we attach great significance to the development of cinematography, to the creation of film *in bringing the people lofty ideals of international friendship, humanism, peace and progress."* [11]

Khrushchev's hottest blast, however, was yet to come. Sunday is no day of rest for the propagandist, and the final payoff on the Fox studio goof waited until the following day in San Francisco.

The Premier was lecturing a group of labor leaders when the opportunity arose for a little needling on the Hollywood outing. The participants in the following dialogue were Paul L. Phillips, president of the United Papermakers and Paperworkers, James B. Corey of the International Union of Electrical Radio and Machine Workers, Walter Reuther of the United Auto Workers, and "our boy." The scene was a dining suite at the Mark Hopkins Hotel.

After considerable badinage with the labor leaders on political and economic matters, the Premier seemed happy and pleased with himself. Quite suddenly, and for no demonstrable reason, he launched into a bouncy burlesque of the absurd dance he had seen at the film studio the day before, flipping up his jacket tail and gyrating his ample posterior. The labor leaders' eyes popped. An explanation was forthcoming immediately:

KHRUSHCHEV: This is a dance in which the girls pull up their skirts. *You're* going to see that. *We* are not. This is what you call freedom—freedom for the girls to show their backsides. To us, it's pornography! The culture of people who want pornography! The culture of people who want pornography! *It's capitalism that makes the girls that way."*

PHILLIPS: Does the Chairman think that girls should be prohibited by law from showing their backsides?

KHRUSHCHEV: There should be a law prohibiting girls from showing their backsides—a *moral* law.

CAREY: I may not see it. I may not want to see it—

KHRUSHCHEV: Your *children* will go to see it!

REUTHER: Perhaps it was a stupid movie—it was stupid of them to show it to you [!!!]. But that has nothing to do with . . . the free flow of ideas between our countries. . . . [and so forth]

"It was immoral," said Mr. K, in summary. "A person's face is more beautiful than his backside. Only people who are over-satiated like such things and similar pornography." [12]

Khrushchev had dared to insult Hollywood, and Hollywood bristled—and when Hollywood bristled, the press (and a battery of press agents) amplified a smallish sound into a roar.[13] The movie colony was clucking, "tsking," "oohing," and "ahing," all quite publicly and openly, behaving like smart alecks in the press, on radio, and on television, and apparently mindless that their inane comments were traveling far and wide.

Ezra Goodman reports the episode in his amusing and realistic book, *The Fifty-Year Decline and Fall of Hollywood*,[14] with suitable sarcasm. The visit was called the "Khrushchev caper" by the film people; *Daily Variety* reviewed it, likening Mr. K to a character actor, now "top banana in Hollywood-land." And there was plenty to laugh at, too—like "the fact that Marilyn Monroe and Liz Taylor were the first to arrive, the first time in years either has been on time," and other cute observations such as, "Phui on Krui!" "Go home, Gaspoden—tell 'em how you invented Monroe!" One columnist was incensed that Mary Pickford hadn't been invited. *Daily Variety* added, "Hollywood has never been the origin of a production of such spectacular proportions and, chances are, never will get a chance to do a remake."

All these trivia were, of course, broadcast to neutral peoples still wondering if they could trust the United States, to countries teetering on the brink of Communist revolution, to satellite nations disillusioned by our lack of support in recent rebellions against the Soviets. As Goodman observes, in normal times the size of the Hollywood press corps equals that of Washington, D.C.; swollen by Khrushchev's visit, this and other media of mass communications gave the wiseacres plenty of publicity.

How did the foreign press react to all of this? As expected, Communist journalists turned Mr. K into a conquering hero, charming everyone in all corners with his winning ways, the American people literally at his feet, demonstrating, as he traveled, the numerous facts of Soviet superiority to a grateful, adoring audience.

The Hollywood gambit was summed up thus in a Soviet book: "The can-can was most likely no accident. Somebody wanted a feeling of resentment to destroy the threads of the cordial and good mutual understanding born in Hollywood between Khrushchev and the American actors. But, of course, this did not and could not happen. Only those who have too poor an opinion of their own artists could expect such a thing." [15] According to the Russians, it was all a dark capitalistic plot; would that it had been nothing more than that instead of execrable judgment.

In other countries the reaction was also what might have been expected. It was marked by bewilderment—even anger —at us for our poor taste and by considerable sympathy for Khrushchev. There was much evidence of a willing ear to listen to what he had to say. The *London Daily Mail's* comment was typical: "We think he had a rough ride in the United

States," it wrote, "and some people treated him offensively. The shocking vulgarity of the Hollywood show was in itself an insult, especially to the Russian leader. So far, in fact, the United States seems to have gone all out to show its *worst* side!" This, from friends! Headlines abroad shouted, "Now lay off K!" "Give him a break," and other admonitions to behave like civilized people.[16]

Columnist Arthur Krock called the shots then and there. On September 22, 1959, he stated in the *New York Times:*

"But it remained for Hollywood to give Mr. Khrushchev his best chances as a propagandist. . . . What a windfall, to one whose thesis is American decadence, was the selection of 'Can-Can' in the making as the apotheosis of American movie skill and taste, while in Moscow they were showing 'Tom Sawyer' "! (Quick on the trigger, Radio Moscow had broadcast a dramatization of the Twain classic and a reading of Hemingway's *Old Man and the Sea* on the fateful day.) Indeed, "we were never lovelier" than on that afternoon when the Premier of the USSR visited Hollywood, California.

From San Francisco, he headed east to Maryland—with stops along the way—to Camp David. A malleable Eisenhower met him, and by the time the TU-104 was ready to take off for Moscow, Khrushchev had done little or nothing to injure his "image" as a sincere peace-maker, a mask he chose to wear as long as it suited his purposes—until he was almost cornered in Geneva in May, 1960, into making real (not propaganda) cold war concessions to the West. The mask fell when Mr. K announced, shocked to the marrow, that an American spy, along with his U-2 reconnaissance airplane, had been bagged in the Soviet Union. But that is another story, and one which will not be told here.

Was the Hollywood incident a major defeat in the cold war, which is largely concerned with manipulating the minds of men? Hardly. But it is one tiny piece in the gigantic jig-saw puzzle we are investigating: the enigma of why our enemies seem so much more adept at the art of mass persuasion than we are.

Incidental to the prime cause of the Hollywood mess—but important in evaluating it—is the fact, as mentioned before, that the United States is an open society. It was opened further than usual by the frantic interest of our mass media in Mr. K's every move. Menus of his breakfast were printed in newspapers, gossip was unearthed about his personal habits, speculation raged about his family life, and the like. Since it was absolutely certain at the outset of the junket that every move on our part would receive exactly the same kind of world-wide scrutiny, it was up to those American officials in charge of arranging Khrushchev's itinerary to exercise wisdom and caution in the desperately serious business of making sure that the smallest opportunity be offered to him for building destructive propaganda. Quite the opposite happened in California—and the results of such poor judgment have added their mite to the beating we have taken in the war of words.

One may sympathize with the overworked, underpaid State Department officials involved here. Nevertheless, the hard-core issue of national and personal survival turns bitter every attempt to excuse their blunders, large or small. Poor judgment, both at home and abroad, can be explained, but must be prevented from happening again.

Proceeding one step further, the prime cause of the incident—and if it had not happened in Hollywood it probably would have happened elsewhere—is the fact that the image of America automatically reflects pretty much what we *are*. And we are—in part at any rate, among many other facets we don't project—the kind of community that Hollywood speaks for:

gaudy, tasteless, and silly. It was perhaps inevitable, then, that at one point or another in his tour, Mr. Khrushchev was bound to run headlong into that aspect of our society and use it as a whipping boy.

The point is, however, that the damage might have been held to a minimum if we had handled his visit more perceptively by showing him happier and more substantial elements of our culture. For we are more than a gaudy, tasteless, and silly people. Our best features are frequently lost in the shuffle. The things for which Hollywood is a typical spokesman have louder voices, jazzier press agents, more push and pull; and they are the ones that most often are heard and served.[17]

True, Khrushchev was shown *some* of our cultural resources. But he was afforded no more than a tiny peek at our museums, colleges, courts of law, municipal operas, community theaters, national parks, schools, and libraries. Little stress was placed upon the remarkable spread of the amenities of civilization to millions of Americans as never before in the history of the world—and unparalleled elsewhere *now*. With the possible exception of Scandinavia, and even granting the wastelands of mediocrity and institutionalized barbarism within our boundaries, we may lay claim to being the most sophisticated and truly humane nation on earth.

Why was all this kept secret from Nikita Khrushchev? Why was *this* view, so easy for so many of *us* to come by, obstructed by female posteriors?

There are many who will never believe that Mr. K came to these shores with any but the most doctrinaire aims, ready to make anti-American propaganda out of each and every opportunity given him. Conceding much or all of this, was it not possible nevertheless to demonstrate to him that capitalism doesn't *need* to be decadent, and that we are a people for

whom significant human values take precedence over tomfool-
ery and the almighty dollar? On that afternoon in September,
it looked as if such a possibility never even entered our minds.

Some would solve this problem of creating a favorable national image for export by decreasing the degree to which we
are an open society. In other words, they would emulate the
Soviet Union's censorship and control of information. Even
President Kennedy has implied that such control is not unthinkable.

Should we attempt this course, we would be faced with a
tragic dilemma. In trying to prevent both our friends and enemies from dwelling too insistently upon our (all too real) defects, we would simultaneously sacrifice one of our major values: our love of freedom of thought and speech and reluctance
to employ coercive tactics against the minds and tongues of
our people. This would be an ironical end result for a nation
nurtured on liberty, and would justly equate us with our totalitarian enemies in the eyes of the world.

Is freedom worth the chance we take—the chance that the
cumulative effect of the Hollywood fiascos of the future will
dangerously disgust and disillusion our allies and fire the furnaces of our antagonists?

It is—if we succeed in reducing this chance, not to the vanishing point (which is impossible), but to the degree that
smart, tough men like Nikita Khrushchev will have a hard
time taking advantage of our weaknesses.

It is—if our responsible citizenry, statesmen, and leaders
of thought and opinion assert themselves and their values. It
is—if Americans at large wake up to the realization that a
richer and profounder spiritual and aesthetic life is going on
in this country than is superficially indicated by the fanfare of
a cheap amusement industry.

In the end, Nikita Khrushchev went back to the Soviet

Union with notable advantages in the cold war, in addition to an enhanced reputation at home. By turns gay, sad, friendly, and at least outwardly furious, he proved more than a match for those who challenged him. With the vast resources both of the Soviet propaganda machine and of American and free-world mass communications media at his command, he sold the world on "co-existence," Russian style, to cloak his clever maneuvers in the diplomatic arena until it suited his geopolitical strategy to wreck the Geneva conference and at least temporarily to dispense with his "peace-maker's mask."

The whole affair is lurid enough to become the plot of a Hollywood film. Unfortunately, it lacks comic relief.

DON'T DRINK THE WATER

They change their clime, not their disposition, who run beyond the sea.

—HORACE, *Epistles* I

The soul is no traveler; the wise man stays at home, and when his necessities, his duties, on any occasion call him from his house, or into foreign lands, he is at home still and shall make men sensible by the expression of his countenance that he goes, the missionary of wisdom and virtue, and visits cities and men like a sovereign and not like an interloper or a valet. . . .

Traveling is a fool's paradise. Our first journeys discover to us the indifference of places. At home I dream that at Naples, at Rome, I can be intoxicated with beauty and lose my sadness. I pack my trunk, embrace my friends, embark on a sea and at last wake up in Naples, and there beside me is the stern fact, the sad self, unrelenting, identical, that I fled from. I seek the Vatican and the palaces. I affect to be intoxicated with sights and suggestions, but I am not intoxicated. My giant goes with me wherever I go.

—RALPH WALDO EMERSON in *Self-Reliance*

IN AN impressive and official-looking document, typical of those which emerge from the United States Government Printing Office,[1] President Eisenhower in 1958 transmitted to the Congress a report prepared in 1956 by his assistant, Clarence B. Randall, retired Chairman of the Board of the Inland Steel Company. In it one finds a baldly stated assumption about the efficacy of tourism and the role of travel in the invasion of ideas from nation to nation which may well be as dubious a proposition as any competent adult has mouthed since Cicero told the Romans that virtue was its own reward.

"Travel is also a vital factor," wrote Mr. Randall, "in the development of that greater international understanding which leads to peace. Travel makes back-fence neighbors of nations. It knits people together, people of separate and strange backgrounds. As strangers become friends through travel, nations must follow. . . . More and more travel by people of the world will reduce the areas of difference between them. Prejudices will soften, and it will become clear that no man at heart really wishes to destroy his fellow man.

"As we seek the political goal of world peace, therefore, we should make the strongest efforts to promote international travel." [2]

There is nothing intrinsically wrong with Mr. Randall's logic—or his motives. The trouble is that he is juggling a number of doubtful *assumptions* with which he starts. The first is that travel, in fact, brings people into contact with one another. The second posits that contact, granted it does take place, yields friendship, communality, and the understanding of common goals. Thirdly, he takes as axiomatic, granted that such understanding is engendered, that the relationships achieved by people on a personal level of operation have a relationship to political activities in international relationships between nations, especially when it comes to the problem of whether or not nations will declare war on each other.

Anyone who has studied the history of our century and thinks for an instant about the cultural and personal links which tie individual Americans to the Germans and Japanese, the Koreans to the Chinese, the Russians to the Poles, the Italians to the French, and the Nicaraguans to the Costa Ricans and Guatemalans has the right to challenge all three of these assumptions with a skeptical "Maybe!"

Undoubtedly, in one way or another, travel broadens the traveler, and it is likely to provide for him healthy insights into the nearly unbelievable variety of ways that men have evolved in adapting themselves to the environment of our planet. Undoubtedly, the sort of contact between people which travel allows does produce *something* in terms of the image that individuals and groups form in their minds of the travelers they see around them.

The vital question involved in all this seeks to ascertain *what* image is produced and whether or not such an image does indeed confirm Mr. Randall's proposition that contact between people of different nations enhances mutual understanding and therefore ramifies into political affairs.

Mr. Randall is, of course, not the only expert who believes it does. In a remarkable article in the *New York Times Magazine* a few years ago,[3] S. I. Hayakawa (a well-known professor and writer who, incidentally, seems to believe that all international, social, and personal problems are the result of "semantic breakdowns" or problems in understanding words and sentences), made the audacious suggestion that we in the United States remove all travel and security restrictions and let all and every Soviet, Red Chinese, or what have you go where they will within our territorial limits for as long as they like. According to Dr. Hayakawa, this simple prescription would eliminate international tension and end the cold war. See us for what we are, he implies, and you can't help but love us.

On the other hand, the popular press has been filled in recent years with articles making a case for the opposite proposition. The term "ugly American" may be applied these days not only to government workers and diplomats, but also to the travelers whom Mr. Randall sees as the instruments of world peace. In a symposium on Americans abroad, newscaster Edward P. Morgan spoke about American tourists who ". . . stubbornly set out for far places . . . , generously strewing little ulcers of ill will along their jet trails. . . . Nor is it realistic to think that we can influence people by flying a gaudy banner of 'Americanism'—whatever that is—and insist that the increasing host of humans in other lands are missing a bet if they don't do things the way we do." [4] C. K. Sulzberger, in the same *New York Times Magazine* that gave a forum to Dr. Hayakawa's unique proposal, wrote about the tendency of Europeans to resist the Americans for "exclusiveness abroad, the tendency of our travelers to 'drink Coca-Cola' among the most magnificent vineyards." [5]

The fear that these gentlemen are articulating is, precisely, the fear that Mr. Randall's assumptions are wrong, that contact does not necessarily yield understanding, that Americans, for the most part, make a poor impression overseas. And this impression, they say, viewing it with alarm, is generalized into a broader image of America at large, her aspirations and her actions in the international arena.

Who is right? Is tourism (and are American tourists) a viable source of good will for the United States in the places where Americans go? Does personal understanding yield a harvest in the relationship between nations? Are tourists good idea invaders and effective persuaders in creating a climate favorable to America in neutral or friendly countries, and do such contacts with hostile ones ease tensions? Or are the naysayers correct? Do Americans make boorish impressions overseas, simply rubbing sore spots of antagonism and stirring up hostility? And does such hostility have a direct relationship to the image that citizens of distant lands have of us, adding fuel to the propaganda furnaces of our antagonists? Is tourism, in fact, a detriment to the diplomatic problem of arranging the kind of mutual agreements between nations which will prevent the present cold war from running hot?

To answer these questions dispassionately, it is necessary, first, to take a look at the typical American tourist. This is a difficult task because, obviously, many different kinds of people travel abroad for many reasons and behave in widely varying ways. But since tourism remains a relative luxury for citizens of the United States, and since the appeals of travel are attractive only to certain and specific kinds of people with certain interests, it is possible to investigate, on the basis of available data, at least some of the inherent possibilities.[6]

First of all, the American who travels abroad is usually a white Caucasian. Few of our 15,000,000 Negroes, 400,000

Indians, or 300,000 Orientals meet the economic requirements necessary to become travelers on foreign soil. Accordingly, foreigners who are interested in members of our racial minorities rarely have an opportunity to meet any of them. The absence of such minorities from American guided tours, common sense reminds us, cannot help but confirm the opinions of those abroad who incline to believe that the good things in American life, particularly those derived from all-important economic pursuits, are denied to members of minority groups.

The largest number of Americans come from our richest, most sophisticated (and, many believe, *atypical*) states: New York and California. All in all, the Northeastern states lead in the production of tourists, with the North Central, Pacific, South Atlantic, South Central, and Mountain states following in that order. As a matter of fact, about six times as many passports are issued in the states of New York, New Jersey, Pennsylvania, Massachusetts, Connecticut, Rhode Island, Maine, New Hampshire, and Vermont combined as in the group composed of Texas, Louisiana, Oklahoma, Tennessee, Alabama, Kentucky, Mississippi, and Arkansas. *And this is the case despite the fact that the population of the former group is only one and one-half times as great as the population of the latter!*

The occupations of the largest number of males who travel abroad are those of skilled or technical workers, salesmen, independent business men, and professional men. And since such a profusion of housewives are found among our tourists, we may conclude that the average peripatetic American travels with his wife. This means that our ambassadors of good will abroad are largely middle class or upper class citizens, employed in relatively skilled and stable positions, who travel with their women, equally upper middle class, and, presumably, of equally stable status. Students, retired folk, teachers,

secretaries, and ministers make up the next occupational categories in the order shown. (It would appear, therefore, that
the conception of enormous hordes of liberated, American
secretaries invading Europe each year and flattening the
grasses of exotic places as they make hanky-panky with swarthy
European gallants, is pretty much a myth. Housewives out-
number secretaries more than five to one, and nearly three
times as many students as secretaries travel abroad.)

The Americans that foreigners see are unquestionably ma-
ture—at least in terms of age. In spite of the publicity given to
Boy Scouts and youth hosteling, only about 10 per cent of our
tourists are under twenty, and about 25 per cent of them are
under thirty. Nearly half are over forty, and the group of traveling oldsters over the age of sixty makes up about 20 per cent
of the total flock of Americans who go overseas in a year.
They comprise, also, the largest single group of Americans
over twenty who travel abroad.

How long do Americans stay overseas? Since most trips
must be compressed within a conventional vacation period, it
is not surprising that about two-thirds of our foreign travelers
stay overseas less than two months and about one-third stay
less than one month, hardly time enough to be extensively
"broadened," and also not much time to develop the kinds of
friendships and attachments discussed in Mr. Randall's document. Whether this is time enough to create a poor impression
of America in the mind of a Frenchman, Russian, or Greek,
we leave the reader to judge.

Why do Americans travel? This is difficult to determine
with any precision, but, in their own judgment, most of them
who are not on business or government missions say they are
traveling for "pleasure." Only minuscule numbers refer to anything like "education," "religion," or an objective other than
to satisfy their footloose instincts.

In selecting countries in which to travel, the American tourist follows a predictable pattern: he goes to the places which are easiest to reach and/or which most resemble the United States of America. The latter penchant leads us to wonder if, perhaps, he prefers to be broadened a bit, but not too much. Such parochialism and search for safety, though, are quite understandable inasmuch as "the comforts of home" are far more likely to be available in places that are most like home. Western Europe and the British Isles are therefore his favorite foreign destinations, followed at a considerable distance by Bermuda and the West Indies (to which he may be drawn by the lure of proximity and cheap liquor), the Far East, South America, Australia and environs, and—trailing way behind—Africa.

In Europe itself the clean, efficient, industrialized (and expensive) nations of West Germany and Switzerland rank first in popularity by a startlingly wide margin over Italy, which is more likely the spiritual and ancestral home of so many Americans. And well over twice as many Americans go to Italy as tour Great Britain, next nation in rank sequence. Following England are France, Spain, Austria, Holland, Belgium, and Denmark in the order mentioned.

One thing is certain, American tourists spread around fabulous amounts of money. During the average year of 1960, 741,000 Americans abroad spent $1,610,000,000 on travel— excluding transportation of all kinds, which if added to the total, would add another $2,380,000,000 for a grand total of about $4,000,000,000.

Apart from transportation, the loot was divided in this manner: a little less than half of it was spent in Europe, while about 14 per cent went to South American, Central American, and Caribbean countries. Canada, Mexico and the rest of the nations of the world shared what was left of the American tourist dollar between them, in what would seem to be a working model of fiscal inequality.

To recapitulate, our typical American tourist fits the following picture in one degree or another: he is from one of the more "sophisticated" or "citified" parts of the USA; he is over forty, has his wife in tow; he is usually a skilled worker, professional man, or business man, comfortably upper middle class and out for a good time. He is on his way to a place where things are neither dramatically nor drastically different from the USA—that is, where he will find flush toilets, doctors, and refrigerators and where he will be able to indulge in his favorite foods and amusements. Regardless of the fact that he is not among the very wealthy, as Americans calculate people of great riches, he has a fantastically large bundle of dollars in his money belt, a book of traveler's checks or a letter of credit, and he will in all probability spend everything he has.

What he knows or does not know about his native land or about the country which is the object of his sojourn, we shall discuss later. It is sufficient for our purposes, at this point, just to look at him.

Regarding the image he creates overseas, this is a moot point. Along with his American passport, he is handed a lot of so-called "travel-tips" and a reminder from the President that "to all the varied peoples of these many countries, you, the bearer of an American passport, represent the United States of America." As travel expert Horace Sutton says, the epistle urges him to behave, "much as a parent might admonish a child before dispatching him to a neighbor's house for a weekend." [7]

What he does after he is dispatched is anybody's guess, and every tourist, travel agent, and armchair diviner takes a shot at the game.[8] Their arguments are documented with personal impressions and opinions which have been conveyed to them in a handful of interviews with foreigners on their own soil from which "selected quotes" are presented. Much of the argumentation merely reveals the political and social views of the various respondents. Little is statistically sound. One gets the impression that much of the "interviewing" was conducted at sidewalk cafes, in cable cars, or on the beaches of resort towns. It might be called a "where-there's-smoke-there's-fire" type of research, and it is difficult—if not impossible—to confirm or refute, because affirming or denying the relevance of the judgments involved is like swatting moonbeams.

The case against American tourists as the prime instrumentality of the supposedly faulty image that foreigners have of us is built on a number of fundamental points, which are repeated in various versions and with differing degrees of emphasis:

First, the American is parochial. He may expect everything in Rome, Athens, or Algeria to be just the same as it was in Podunk. Second, he is vain and superior about being an American. Third, his Americanism has an evangelical flavor which implies that all foreign problems can be solved by the application of Yankee "know-how." Fourth, he dresses in a manner that is offensive to the local population. Fifth, he is loud and uncouth, and his children are undisciplined. Sixth, he tends to isolate himself from local life, drives ugly, unwieldy automobiles, and reads only American made or Americanized publications. Seventh, he makes no effort whatsoever to learn the language of the country he is visiting, and expects, as a natural right, that he will be spoken to in English. Eighth, he makes no effort to apprise himself of the historic, social, political, or cultural climate of the country he visits and is strangely proud of his ignorance. Ninth, he is a frenetic and unimpressed "doer" of cities, museums, ruins, night clubs, a sort of culture glutton who neither understands much of what he sees nor stands still long enough to absorb any of it or its meaning. Tenth, he is filthy rich and insists on spending his loot as ostentatiously as possible. Overtipping and overpaying for everything, he makes economic life for foreign residents difficult as he drives up prices for goods and services. Eleventh, he is a sorry spectacle in his overeagerness to be loved and admired. Twelfth (and if some of these charges appear to be at odds with one another, we cannot help that; consistency does not seem to be the strong point of this bill of particulars), he is excessively cagey and insecure, giving the impression that he believes all the "damn foreigners" are out to fleece him of his *baksheesh* and he is fair game for any and all con men and sharpers. Thirteenth, his taste in food and drink is uncivilized. Having become neurotically accustomed to canned, prefabricated, poorly cooked, desiccated meals, he is constitutionally incapable of enjoying the delights of a foreign cuisine, particularly the grandeurs of English cooking. Fourteenth, he is cocky, ostentatious, ungentlemanly, disrespectful of local customs and conventions. Fifteenth, he is adolescent and uncultivated, and he spreads abroad the worst, not the best, of American culture—with his comic strips, bebop addiction, and hipster ways. Sixteenth, he is brash and just plain noisy. Seventeenth, he has not mastered the art of holding his liquor. Eighteenth, he does not respect the quaint plumbing conventions of foreign lands and finds devices like the stand-up toilet a most constipating experience. And so forth. It is quite possible to play a number of variations on these eighteen points and apply them to a wide range of activities.

There is no doubt that this viewpoint is a pretty negative one, and, even granting some truth to all the charges therein, it is unquestionably overdrawn. Nor has it gone unanswered, although defending the American tourist in print these days seems to have less psychological appeal than slapping him around. The defense[9] seems to rest mostly on the observation that Americans are neither better nor worse than any other kind of tourist, and if they stick out like sore thumbs when they go abroad, that is because travelers in strange places always stick out like sore thumbs. The turbaned Indians one sees in mid-town New York or the native African potentates in their tribal garb have a way of attracting attention in Washington, D.C., but they are rarely blamed for it, nor does anyone find it a very serious matter that they do not rush off to John David or the Adam Hat stores in order to haberdash themselves *à l'Amerique*. That they may practice Yogi, swill yogurt, compound curries over their Sterno stoves, and turn up their noses at the delights of hamburgers and hot-dogs is hardly an index of parochialism. In all probability, these cross-cultural *gaucheries* will be considered by Americans as "quaint."

The American matron with her tight brassière looks silly, of course, in a market-place in Tahiti, but infinitely less silly than if she "went native" and stripped to the waist for a jaunt around town. Traveling is an arduous, difficult exercise in stamina at its best, and the fact that the American does not attempt, like Proteus, to blend into his environment, so that he will be *gemütlich* in a German beer garden, *sympatico* at a bull fight, and *sympathique* on the Rue de la Paix, is not only understandable, it is inevitable. That he is indeed an American and behaves like an American—which means that he displays both the better and worse aspects of our culture—is neither strange nor unexpected. How else would one have him behave? Most certainly, the reply continues, some Americans make twerps out of themselves, but there is no shortage of local twerps in any of the places Americans visit to give them tough competition. The tourist is an especially vulnerable soul and attracts attention to himself by merely being "himself"—

away from home, in the place he finds himself. Whatever elements in his nature are unattractive to foreign eyes will be noticed and magnified. Similar considerations apply to Russians touring the American Midwest, French students on a hiking trip through Italy, or Bolivian sailors on shore leave in Seattle, Washington.

There is something grim and discouraging about those American tourists who lean over backward in order *not* to appear to be Americans. Slinking around in burnooses and fezzes, they grunt a *patois* they assume to be the local language, eat themselves into dyspepsia with foods cooked under sanitary conditions to which the locals (but not they) are immune, pride themselves on "living like the natives," and accomplish little more than giving themselves hives and exercises in stoicism. This is fine for masochists, but it is difficult to believe that these specimens—usually physical-education types or long-in-the-tooth Boy Scouts, hairy knees protruding from walking shorts, wobbling and sweating under their knapsacks, and meticulously counting their change—lend much dignity to the American abroad.

Interesting to consider is the case of the tourist from overseas who comes to the United States. We assume that he will sponge up our ways by nature, and so we do very little to ease his way or to allow him to preserve whatever distinctive cultural characteristics he displays. And few overseas tourists choose (or can afford) to visit our shores for this very reason —because we do *not* provide them with the scope to be themselves and to insulate themselves from the elements in our culture which they might find either strange or uncomfortable.

Back in 1960 President Eisenhower launched a "Visit the USA Year" that was something of a colossal flop for a number of reasons. If an incipient tourist unravels the welter of red tape that makes getting a tourist's visa for travel in

America about as easy as getting into the Union League Club, and if he can worm past the eagle eye of our immigration officials whose arbitrariness is a by-word, he has overcome only some initial hurdles. Problems galore remain to plague him, not the least of which may be the cost of living in the USA. No doubt this will give grave pause to many a foreign traveler as he makes his vacation plans.[10]

Once he is on our shores, he is faced with an unbelievable shortage of guide-books in his own language, can obtain only a paltry handful of confusing street maps, and is offered just a few packaged, guided tours, which in any case are often "only for Americans" and hardly ever for non-English speaking visitors. Our Travelers' Aid Society does its manly best for them, but by and large, they are ignored and allowed to shift for themselves. To cap the climax, most of them find touring America dreadfully expensive because very little, if anything is done for them in giving them preferential exchange rates (received by American tourists in many nations of the world), relief from local taxes on consumer goods they mean to take out of the country, or special transportation prices. American travelers get far better treatment in England, where one of the major attractions for them is a dollar value made as reasonable as possible.

It is no surprise, therefore, that the number of foreign tourists who come to our shores for pleasure is the merest of trickles—numbers as small as 53,000 each year from England (the largest batch), 12,000 from France, as few as 5,000 apiece from countries as wealthy and progressive as Switzerland and Sweden. Our government is remarkably candid about this problem. In a Department of Commerce *Bulletin* dated April, 1961,[11] we find the following statements:

> Our reception of the traveler at the United States port of entry leaves much to be desired in comparison with other coun-

tries. Considerable thought should and is being given to improving our customs handling of the arriving traveler. . . .

We are far behind other nations of the world in the use of other languages as a sign of hospitality and welcome. The most difficult problem of the average foreign traveler and the strongest psychological block he has to traveling to the U.S.A. lies in the problem of communication. He has been told, and he knows, that the average American citizen is not bilingual, and there is little we have done at airports, piers, railroad stations, or within major cities to ease his problem.

Our restaurants, hotels and other services which come in daily contact with the foreign visitor are not skilled in the same service standards as a traveler meets in Europe.

And so forth.

The reasons, therefore, why American tourists overseas seem to operate under the cloud of a never-ending inferiority complex are probably related to the fact that they see so very few foreign travelers in America, and thus cannot recognize their own awkwardness as the inevitable plight of the traveler anywhere. It is quite possible that there is a great deal less wrong with the average European's image of the American tourist than the American tourist's image of what a tourist is or should be! Having seen so few models of foreign tourists in action on his own home grounds, he has few guide lines by which to judge his own behavior—or to know what to expect from the behavior of others. It is probably the "role of the tourist" and what is, or will be, expected of him that bewilders him most.

If there is one element that unquestionably characterizes the American overseas it is naïveté—a naïveté generalized to cover so many areas of existence that it smells a good deal like raw stupidity.

The one type of traveling American that might be calculated to be most aware of the problems of tourism, as well as the responsibility assumed by tourists in representing their native land, is probably the American college student. Yet, a study conducted in 1958 at Syracuse University shows without a doubt that such expectations are not justified in fact.

American college students represent something of an élite of young Americans. Most Americans do not go to college, and the assumption is justified that those who have resources for foreign travel in addition to funds to meet their tuition must be, on the average, pretty well-heeled—even granting student discounts on foreign travel, educational grants, and the austerity with which students seem to be able to live overseas. All in all, therefore, we are hardly justified in considering them "average" Americans in any sense of the word. They are the cream of our crop, or our crop does not have a cream.

The highly reputable report [12] mentioned above indicates that 70 per cent of this random sample of students who were departing for foreign climes *either were unable to speak the language* of the country for which they were headed or spoke it in an awkward and incomprehensible manner. What's more, when asked questions about the basic and simple history or geography of Europe, such as, "In which city would you find the Louvre?" *63 per cent of them were rated (charitably) as superficially or poorly oriented.*

In addition—and what is perhaps more shocking—they were asked eleven questions about the United States including, "In what year is the next Presidential election?" and "About how many people live in the United States today?" To these brain-teasers, *64 per cent were rated as superficially or poorly oriented.*

Naïveté may, indeed, be too gentle a term to describe our unofficial ambassadors abroad, and if this is the baggage our students bring with them, can you imagine how our present-day Babbitts fare? One is led to wonder how successfully our institutions of education have been in preparing the young for the real challenges which life has in store for them—challenges derived from citizenship in a world which requires living on many levels, not only with one's family, community, and fellow employees, but with the harsh realities of international conflict.

Of course, students and tourists are not the only Americans overseas, and whatever impression they do or do not make upon the minds of people in other nations, the latter will relate their image of the typical American only in part to the pleasure seekers. The American serviceman has long been an intercultural enigma. One of the present writers remembers hearing an Algerian woman lament that American soldiers are barbarians; the Germans who preceded them into North Africa, she claimed, were real gentlemen! What price gentility! Anyone who has been exposed to soldiers of other nations—particularly Turks and Russians—usually has pleasant things to say about the American military man. True, his interest in foreign culture when abroad may manifest itself chiefly in the effects of distilled volatile fluids and the charms of young females. This is not peculiar to the American soldier. Probably it is characteristic of military life the world over. On the credit side of the ledger, the American soldier tends to detach himself from the culture of the nation in which he is stationed, and, while he is frequently criticized for his PX economy and his tendency to create "little Americas" around himself, this is probably a proclivity preferable to a passion for throwing himself bull-like into local foreign customs, institutions, and amusements. The American soldier overseas, considering the political and military burden he has been forced to carry in most of his posts, as well as his cross-cultural problems, has, by and large, not fared badly, even in such outposts as Iceland, where negative Icelandic attitudes toward minority-group servicemen rankled his democratic sensibilities, and he was for a long time consistently given the cold shoulder.

Perhaps the military has a taste for the abundant life, especially where officers and their wives and children are concerned,[13] but one must remember that in exchange for their income (and this is not lavish by the standards of an American business man) American military personnel have been assigned to a formidable tour of duty in alien lands. Many overseas soldiers have mastered technical occupations which could command healthy salaries, considerable comfort, and security back home. They are also faced with the dull, dehumanizing bureaucracy of service life—but there is no need to repeat the story of Captain Queeg in *The Caine Mutiny*.

As to other non-tourist traveling Americans, they achieve their ends with varying degrees of success—depending on where they go and what they do. If most reports can be trusted,[14] our visiting Congressmen fare poorly as representatives of the USA, but fortunately they are few and far between and the purposes behind their junkets are a standing joke at home and abroad. Standing jokes are hard to take seriously.

The "ugly Americans"—our government workers and their technical assistants who venture abroad and do not adapt to conditions as they find them—have been the victims of so much rhetoric and indignation that they will receive little attention here. Needless to say, it is results that count, and many, if not most, of the recent technical accomplishments of the free world are directly attributable to American technical aid. Even within the Soviet Union (largely as a consequence of our sympathies with the Russians during the 1930's and immediately after World War II) there was some dependence upon American expertise. When technicians or government workers pull a boner, they tend to pull a big and important one, but how the incompetence of a few is overbalanced by the competence, efficiency, and dedication of many is a story yet to be told.

American business men are generally respected overseas, and probably make a better impression than any other single group of travelers. At least this is true in capitalist countries. In the first place, they do their homework. They know foreign markets, sales potentials, transportation possibilities, labor scales and problems. In the second place, they tackle their jobs in a "no-nonsense" way that is difficult not to admire. Third, they have a reputation for scrupulous business honesty; they live up to the letter of their contracts and keep their word, even on a verbal basis. To many non-Americans, schooled in a less precise and exacting business ethic than that which prevails in the United States, American business men are indeed remarkable in their attention to detail and probity regarding commercial matters.

Although the American business man is no paragon of virtue in the eyes of all foreigners, at least he is viewed as meticulous and efficient. As more than one observer has indicated, the sincerest form of flattery he has received is the tendency for foreign men of commerce to imitate both his "style" and his methods, his organization and operation. Even business men representing state interests in Communist countries have begun to ape the American way of doing business.

So-called "cultural exchanges" [15] also seem to constitute a breath of fresh air in an otherwise murky situation, and, oddly enough, seem to go on with undiminished vigor even during international crises between nations. In a sense, they divert the mind from major problems involved in international relations. When a Bolshoi Ballet troupe plays in New York to popular acclaim or when "Porgy and Bess" creates a sensation in Moscow, at worst the "image" of the exporting nation will not be damaged, and under certain circumstances it may be helped. For the record, in 1960 we sent abroad seventy-seven such projects to the Soviet Union, twenty-seven to Poland, eight to Hungary, and five to Rumania, and their rate of flow seems amazingly consistent in recent years.

When cultural exchanges work well, they work very well. In 1961, for instance, the Department of State sponsored an overseas tour of the American Repertory Company with such stars as Helen Hayes, Leif Erickson, and Helen Menken, performing in "The Skin of Our Teeth," "The Glass Menagerie," and "The Miracle Worker." The company toured extensively in Europe, the Middle East, and Latin America, and most observers agree that, despite bewilderment at the expressionistic obscurities in "The Skin of Our Teeth," the tour was a success—both in interpreting one facet of American culture for foreign intellectuals and observers and in the exportation of an unusually attractive and personable group of Americans to represent us abroad. Wrote the *Washington Post and Times Herald:*

> This State Department sponsored tour has done more good for less money than anything the U.S. has undertaken with foreign aid funds. Every single ambassador without exception reported that this company has created more good will and ignited more warmth than anything this country ever has done abroad. People in foreign lands respond to such a visit with far more personal warmth, identification, and admiration than to a platoon of stiff-necked diplomats and visiting Congressmen junketing their way around the world. One foreign diplomat is quoted as saying: "You send some pretty ignorant people over here at times. They embarrass us with their naïveté and arrogance. But this company of talented American actors has not created one incident, has never said one word out of line anywhere. They have been a treasure for the U.S. and are devoted intelligent American representatives." [16]

While Senators carped about the high salaries of some of the performers, the tour was an inexpensive venture, considering its results: the European and Near Eastern part cost the government $550,000, while another $450,000 was spent to take the company to South America. Projects like these boil down to an economical and effective way to put our best foot forward overseas on both the cultural and personal levels.[17] Certainly such tours give foreigners a chance to see many aspects of American life and offer them evidence that American motion pictures do not tell the full story about life and culture in the USA.

Most heartening was the passage by Congress of the Mutual Fund Educational Cultural Exchange Act of 1961 [18] and the appointment of an Advisory Commission to the President in the implementation of what appears to be a serious effort to effectuate more programs of this sort.[19] While the act itself offers nothing new or startling in American policy in regard to cultural exchange, it does set about to "expand, strengthen and better define" [20] our rather tentative attempts at exporting samples of American culture overseas. It is designed at the same time to stimulate listening to and looking at similar offerings from other nations.

Benny Goodman and Louis Armstrong may not represent the finest flower of American culture, but it is hard to see how they can do us anything but good in militating against some of the more unflattering stereotypes of American life, values, and art. While the choice of artists we have sent to other countries has been criticized, people overseas are no more likely to generalize hastily after viewing these performances than that Americans will conclude that Russia is a nation of acrobats on the basis of one exposure to the Ukrainian National Dance troupe.

While cultural exchanges can backfire, and while it is of

course necessary that considerable judgment be exercised as to exactly *what* facets of our cultural life we expose overseas, it takes no stroke of genius to observe that a concert pianist or a company performing "My Fair Lady" presents a healthy picture of some very expert American artists doing what they do best. Most certainly, they speak well for us. On the other hand, no depths of perception are necessary to see that our exports of Western movies, canned TV shows, and rock 'n' roll do *not*.

As to the newest exponents of the virtues of America—President Kennedy's Peace Corps—any definitive statement as to how they contribute or will contribute to the image which Americans project overseas will probably have to wait years for the final returns to come in—if we can know even then. Without doubt there will be much scuttlebutt and conjecture, both by enthusiasts and detractors of the organization, and examples of success and failure will be discussed and publicized. But reliable statements in regard to the way in which the Peace Corps spreads abroad the finer aspects of American life will await the judgment of history. It is quite impossible to predict this eventuality from the perspective of the moment.

All of which brings us to a conclusion, difficult to accept by those who are looking for simple answers to complex questions and to whom the world and its worries are IBM cards on which can be stamped "yes," "no," or "maybe."

Underlying the problem of the image that other nationals have of us and the way in which they regard our tourists, students, government workers, technical experts, Congressmen, and Peace Corpsmen is a fundamental series of realities, which lead right to the heart of the new frontiers of international communication and the problems of mass persuasion on a global basis. And these realities apply to the sweet young thing from Montana absorbing culture in the Tate Galleries as well as to the bloated, boozing, butter-and-egg man screeching at the showgirl doxies of Montparnasse to "take it off and make it bounce." They apply to the wife of an American soldier who feels she must feed her children Wheaties for breakfast no less than to the American husband from Iowa who is shocked at the employment of female attendants in Continental men's rooms.

First, it must be understood that attitudes toward foreigners, tourists, or aliens anywhere—at any time or any place—*have little to do with the behavior of the tourists.* Granted, certain extremes of behavior like the violation of serious local taboos, rape, and murder can (and do) cause trouble for national groups on foreign soil, but fortunately such instances are rare. No matter how ignorant a traveler may be of local customs, only a moron can disregard the basic cultural ground rules of existence abroad, so obvious are they in the general tenor of life. The tourist will make errors and unquestionably will occasionally look like a fool. But that brings us to another point: the hard fact that nationals almost everywhere in the world are unbelievably tolerant of the "crazy" behavior of visitors. In fact, they seem to expect it, and, if the situation warrants it, are quick to take prudent action to prevent abuses —womenfolk, family treasures, and the wine supply get locked away when the invaders come.

This is because the tourist, the foreigner, the alien looks like an *Ausländer* almost by definition—a non-conforming fool, an *idiot.* He *is* an idiot, in the original sense of the Greek word: one who does not participate in the culture, values, mores, and traditions of the host nation. No matter where he goes, he calls attention to himself, and no matter what he does he is certain at one time or another, the laws of chance being what they are, to do the wrong thing. This is a quality generic to his fate as a stranger and outsider who has come to a place not to participate in its social or economic life, but to observe it and (one hopes) learn from it. The Urdu in Times Square, the Thai in Leicester Square, the Korean in Moscow, and the Canadian in Cairo all share this fate, and the only way to prevent it from occurring may be to force them all to stay home.

For better or worse, then, whatever attitudes or opinions local people have of the tourist will be formed more or less irrelevantly to what the tourist does or does not do. If the local population wants to regard the tourist as an incompetent, a misfit, or an uncivilized oaf whose values are askew and whose behavior is silly and boorish, it has plenty of scope for the formation of such an opinion on the basis of the specific behavior of specific tourists. If, on the other hand, local people want to regard the tourist as salt of the earth, benign and friendly, they can do this also by allowing for cross-cultural differences or interpreting eccentric behavior in a sanguine way.

Japanese tourists, for example, are almost pathologically addicted to taking photographs—far more so than Americans, Frenchmen, or Englishmen. (A Japanese visitor to an Eastern University who had a lengthy conversation recently with one of the authors took his photograph at the end of the discussion as a record of the meeting and to impress it on his memory!) Now let us imagine two Japanese gentlemen assiduously photographing the Golden Gate Bridge from every conceivable angle. In 1941 they would have been regarded as "damned spies" and "nosey Japs." Their act would have been justifiably judged as sneaky, suspicious and dangerous. In 1963 the same act would be regarded merely as the colorful behavior of congenial Orientals, a harmless display of a quaint culture trait.

As another example, consider British attitudes toward American tourists today and British criticisms of American ostentatiousness, loudness of speech, barbarity of culture, lack of interest in tradition. Upon consideration, one can see clearly how these attitudes reproduce on the personal or microcosmic level, not an English attitude toward individual decorum, but rather attitudes toward the United States vis-à-vis England on the *political-international* level. That is, they have less to do with the behavior of American tourists than they have to do with political, economic, and military matters. Look at their equivalents when writ large: individual ostentatiousness becomes America's gaudy wealth; individual loudness of speech becomes America's powerful voice in international affairs; American barbarity of culture becomes the infiltration of an élite culture in England by forms derived from American life and her mass media of communication; America's lack of interest in tradition becomes her unwillingness to indulge in traditional diplomatic compromises with her enemies. And so on.

For the plain truth is that, as regards the image of Americans overseas, attitudes of foreigners are a function, pure and simple, of their social and political attitudes and are only slightly (or sometimes not at all) contingent upon the behavior of the Americans. In other words, *individual impressions follow and are conditioned by general attitudes*. It is in much the same way that you or I, having crystallized our dispositions toward, say, the Ku Klux Klan as negative, destructive and uncivilized, are almost certain to regard the individual Klansman as generally a negative, destructive and uncivilized individual, no matter what he may say or do on a specific occasion. One has only to consider our attitude here in America to individual Germans in the period from 1935 to 1945 and contrast it with our attitude toward them today. Yet, as *individuals,* the "Germans" have changed not a whit in the time between.

This does not mean that we can afford to send boors, idiots, and hoods abroad. While the American image is related to the hard-core factors noted above, fuel can always be added to a fire, and there is little sense in taking even the slightest risk where matters of such importance are at stake. While an "ambassador of good will," consciously striving to be loved in a place where his breed is hated, will produce few results to vindicate his efforts, it is conceivable that an unfriendly or foolish ambassador will confirm a viewpoint hostile to his cause and bring about what social psychologists call a "precipitation" of attitudes, which will be all but impossible to change later on. On no account must we underemphasize the risks here!

Certain positive steps can be taken (and, to a degree, are being taken by our government and by private agencies, but hardly as yet on an adequate scale) to enable American tourists in foreign countries to derive more pleasure from their travels and to allow them to reap the dividend of a worthy representation of the United States.

Perhaps the most interesting of these programs up to now is ex-President Eisenhower's "People to People" campaign, launched in 1956. In Ike's words, it attempted to encourage servicemen abroad to "represent us all in bringing assurance to the hard-core factors noted above, fuel can always be tion . . ." [21]; and, in a special issue of *Yank,* the Army weekly, various suggestions were made, such as: "Natural Contacts Are Important," "Learn The Language," "Moderation Is Essential," "Your Family Can Help, Too." Since slogans have some bearing on action, we may look forward to continued improvement of the image created by our military personnel.

Taking a leaf from the book of the "People to People" campaign, let us outline a program for more enjoyable travel coupled with the goal of spreading a better understanding of America throughout the world:

1. By means of passport restrictions, or agreements on the part of travel agents, keep American pleasure-seeking tourists away from countries where their chances for a pleasant sojourn are nil. No matter how Americans behave in such countries, they are bound to create a poor impression because the economic, political, military, and cultural cards are stacked against them. Measures of this kind must be delicately handled, and should not be interpreted as blanket restrictions on the right to travel.

2. Discover and exploit the most painless and efficient means of informing every American who leaves our shores of the immediate social, political, and cultural problems he will face as an American in every country he will visit.

3. Supply the American tourist with a brief review of the history and traditions of each country he intends to visit.

4. Make every effort to familiarize the American going overseas with the vital facts relating to *American* government, history, and policy. He should have *at least as much understanding of our past roots and our governmental procedures as is required of an alien before the latter is permitted to assume American citizenship.* The prospective tourist should also be informed of the basics of our present foreign policies and our economic status in the world today. The pamphlet, *Americans Abroad; Questions You'll Be Asked About Your Country,* published by the American Council for Nationalities

Service in New York City, is a good beginning in this direction.

5. If instruction is carried on properly and regularly, a basic *speaking* familiarity with a foreign language—even Chinese or Malay—can be provided easily and quickly for anyone with an IQ over 80. A minimum vocabulary of 500 to 1,000 words in the major tongues of the countries to be visited (requiring no more than one week's part-time study if done right) should be strongly encouraged in every tourist over the age of twelve. This suggestion, however, is difficult to act upon because it raises a host of questions regarding the failure of American methods of education. The authors grant that the idea of American tourists acquiring foreign vocabularies is hardly likely to be taken seriously at the present writing, but ask whether quickie foreign language classes on ocean liners and in trans-Atlantic airplanes, employing records and tape recordings and the latest audio-visual devices, are out of the question? Come to think of it, they might turn out to be a more pleasurable way of conquering motion sickness than conventional diversions like wide-screen movies and shipboard gossip.

Are these suggestions limitations upon free travel and traditional American liberties? If they are, then so are the forms we fill out to get our passports, the passports themselves, and the injunctions stamped therein not to travel where our government cannot guarantee our safety. Obviously, the right to travel does not include license to do as one pleases; the tourist has obligations and responsibilities which neither he nor the nation he represents can afford to shirk.

Nothing will stop the tourist boom as long as Americans have money burning holes in their pockets. But is it not also the duty of our government, travel agents, and others to dramatize the nature and significance of the responsibilities implicit in a decision to take the grand tour for this year's vacation? The idea that the privilege to go where you like requires your good behavior when you get there is hardly so complex that it is beyond the capacity of an average American to understand. Let's spread the news!

BANG, BANG—YOU'RE DEAD

I meet people occasionally who think that motion pictures, the product that Hollywood makes, is merely entertainment, has nothing to do with education. That's one of the darndest fool fallacies that is current. When I was a motion picture editor on the Chicago Daily News *we used to report what was a four-handkerchief picture as distinguished from the two-handkerchief picture. Anything that brings you to tears by way of drama does something to the deepest roots of your personality. All movies good or bad are educational, and Hollywood is the foremost educational institute on earth, an audience that runs into an estimated 800 million to a billion. What, Hollywood's more important than Harvard? The answer is, not as clean as Harvard, but nevertheless, farther reaching.*

—CARL SANDBURG (quoted by Edward R. Murrow) [1]

IDEAS do not travel in a vacuum. Like electricity, they need a medium through which to go: air, water, or copper wire for current; printed words, pictures, or voices for thoughts.

America exports ideas through many channels. The range of media, the sweep of expression, the sheer bulk of this traffic —all are astounding, largely because we as an open, free-enterprise society, have never believed in rigid controls on what we send overseas in the way of thoughts and opinions. The market has been one which seems to seek its own level of saturation, dictates its own rate of flow and content. Every man is in business for himself. Represented are private enterprise, government, educational and other institutions. Everyone sends abroad, to friends and enemies alike, what he pleases, subject to two qualifications; first, whether or not his ideas will be *accepted* for dissemination, and second, whether or not he believes the export of these ideas will, in one manner or another, be *profitable* for him.

As to whether or not this profusion of voices and *mish-mash* of ideation is good or bad for the United States, its future, its diplomatic position, and its relationships with other

123

nations, the reader must judge for himself. Let us here listen to some of the voices, find out for whom they speak, and consider what they are saying.

Assigning the greatest share of blame for a poor image of the United States abroad to the motion picture industry (and its enormous export of Hollywood-made films) has been an indoor sport for at least thirty years.[2] These attacks have been by no means periodical, but rather have gone on in peace and war, good times and bad, and seem irrelevant in their intensity to the ups and downs on the diplomatic front.

A recent criticism is typical. Neither better nor worse than its prototypes, it argues pretty much from conventional assumptions.[3] It is written by a Marianist Brother who has had extensive experience in Latin America. On the basis of his observations, American movies are either "Westerns, gangster films, rock 'n' roll musicals [or] girlie revelations. There are few movies showing normal American life. As a result Latin Americans have a tremendously distorted notion of life in the United States." [4]

Continuing in this vein, the argument intensifies without becoming much more elaborate. "What tragic irony!" he writes. "While the USSR cleverly misrepresents itself, highlighting the noblest aspects of Soviet life and hiding the Communist falsification of values, bemused Uncle Sam lounges at his TV set and lets Hollywood and TV emphasize the tawdry, the sensational, and the sordid in American life. . . . The more educated and responsible Latin Americans, while they may enjoy the Hollywood product, deplore its effects on their people. Until recently juvenile delinquency in the form of roving teen-age gangs was completely unknown in Chile. But the worst elements of Chilean youth have learned from United States movies the jungle tactics of their Northern cousins. A large segment of Chilean youth affect the sophisticated eccentricity of James Dean, from ducktails to pegged pants. Pseudo-Marilyn Monroes hip their way along Santiago streets. Elvis Presley has squirmed his shaky interpretations of rock 'n' roll into the imaginations of Spanish-American teen-agers. . . . Many films which perform a function at home by focusing attention on such social problems as racial injustice only play into the hands of Communists who would slander us abroad. Is there not, then, some way for our State Department to control the export of United States-made movies, eliminating those that show us as crime-mongers, women worshippers, and lynchers of Negroes?" [5] And so it goes.

Unquestionably, American films have a formidable influence abroad; even the most ardent defenders of the *status quo* do not deny this. Neither do they gainsay the fact that the foreign "image" of America is somehow related to these films. It is the nature of both influence and image which is in dispute.

We export movies on a grand scale.[6] In fact, most films made in America are shown *somewhere* overseas. Taken together, our movies gross only an average of about 50 per cent of their revenue from domestic distribution, and so overseas exhibition constitutes a vital, life-or-death market, the difference between profit and loss in an industry with enormous overheads and production costs.

There is no control in law regarding what pictures may or may not be exported. On an informal basis, however, one or another government agency, charged with international affairs, will let its views be known directly or indirectly to the producers or their organization, the Motion Picture Association of America, when it feels that a particular film will do damage in a foreign country. It will neither coerce nor threaten, but its advice is frequently listened to with care by producers, ever fearful of restrictive legislation.

American films are patronized heavily abroad.[7] Along

with India and Japan, America produces the greatest part of the films made in the world today.[8] The MPAA seal was given to 211 films in 1960, 122 of which were local products, and the remainder of them represented American interests in one way or another. Hollywood movies command a large share of the world movie-going market, varying from nation to nation as to the percentage of American films that exhibitors are permitted to screen. In Britain, exhibitors must offer one British film out of three movies shown. The proportion also depends on the size and health of the local film industry and various economic and cultural factors such as our reluctance to do business with Iron Curtain countries and vice-versa.

Some authorities hold that criticism of American films heard abroad is merely a reflection of anti-American bias and rarely relates to the films themselves. At any rate, one usually hears criticism of Hollywood more from highbrows and intellectuals than from spokesmen for middle and lower class interests, and rejection of American movies is pretty much in one-to-one agreement with the degree of rabid nationalism on foreign soil.

As noted above, the films certainly have their effects, for better or worse. A recent colorful picture story in *Esquire* magazine[9] demonstrates beyond doubt the influence of Southern California on the Tokyo film industry. The article shows old Japanese prints in juxtaposition with sultry photos of bosomy Nipponese movie actresses, like the formidably endowed Mie Hama and Kyoko Izumi, and Japanese "cowboy" star Jyoh Shishido. It's a pretty sure bet that wherever the arm of Hollywood has reached overseas it has scratched culture —and caused an irritation of some kind—while the Hollywood ideal, or lack of it, has replaced older traditions and values in art, morality, and ethics.[10]

Spokesman for the American movie industry in this conflict

of interests is Eric Johnston, high-salaried president of the MPAA and polished front man for the Hollywood producers who get (and stay) healthy and wealthy from the unrestricted flow of films abroad. Just about every year a document[11] emerges from Mr. Johnston's office which denies that American films are a pernicious influence on the American image abroad.

Such documents start with a preamble like the following:

> Clearly, the United States motion picture is an effective ambassador in the other nations of the world. Among all media of mass communication, the American film ranks first in universal appeal. . . . [Over the years] it has lost none of its popularity and has gained immeasurable prestige.
>
> These observations are borne out in comment after comment from country after country. These latest survey responses show, in fact, a greater awareness and a deeper appreciation of the cultural, educational, and social contributions being made by our motion pictures abroad.

Johnston then follows up by providing "prestige" quotes from leading authorities on the excellence of Hollywood films and the magnificence of the work they are doing in interpreting American goals and ideals abroad. Among the luminaries he cites in the current document are Berlin's Mayor Willy Brandt; film-maker Sir J. Arthur Rank; Sir Alexander B. King, the British Minister of Education; a newspaper publisher and celebrities from Indonesia, India, Brazil, Guanabara, and so forth. (One notices the preoccupation with authorities in England and Brazil, both countries where America's good name has been said to be tarnishing and the movies have come in for their share of the blame.) Short quotations from each source seem to indicate that there are many notable citizens who would take issue with the words of our Marianist brother, quoted previously—particularly citizens whose welfare depends in any strategic way upon the economic health and welfare of American business, of which our film industry constitutes a sizable fraction.

Next year's document to emerge from the desk of Mr. Johnston will undoubtedly replicate the present one, although it is to Mr. J's credit that in 1958 he *did* present the results of a survey with occasional reference to statistics. The "survey" was, as far as can be determined, made by Mr. Johnston himself, and he gives no indication in the document either of who was asked what or why anyone was asked. This does not prevent him from making such flat statements as, "The reports show that 85 per cent of our films create 'a favorable attitude toward the United States.' Approximately ten per cent create an attitude neither favorable or unfavorable. About five per cent tended to create an unfavorable attitude 'toward the United States.' " And so forth.

Mr. Johnston's bland pronouncements, however, serve an important purpose for the American movie industry, ever vulnerable to attacks—both responsible and irresponsible—as to the influence films have abroad. And these attacks come from many quarters.

For instance, on November 5, 1961, Edward R. Murrow, quondam CBS newscaster and reporter and by then head of the United States Information Agency, spoke at a forum dinner about Hollywood fat cats. His talk, right or wrong, demonstrated his well-known grit in bucking powerful private interests, for his position vis-à-vis the industry's glad-hander, Mr. Johnston, could not have been more directly opposed.

Mr. Murrow noted his unfamiliarity with the film business and the impropriety of telling men how to run their business, and made other conventional obeisances to modesty, but he followed through with strong stuff which must have shivered some timbers on Malibu beach. Without comment, these extracts explain themselves and clearly put Murrow in the camp of our Marianist:

> Going even further, the impact of movies on illiterate societies can be profound. If a man cannot read or write, seeing and experiencing are his only paths of knowledge. Many an African owes his present level of general knowledge to foreign films. For example, in four West African cities among those who cannot read almost 40 percent are regular movie-goers. These people learn what they never knew before, and they also learn to advance what they already know.
>
> But doesn't this disturb you? Pause a moment, and consider the proposition that whatever these people know of the United States they have largely learned from Hollywood's product. Are you satisfied with the way you have pictured America as a place to live? I shall resist the temptation of adopting the critic's garb and reciting an indictment of alleged movieland ills. But I shall make one comment. There are many people abroad who think that Chicago is still wracked by gang warfare, that the West is still wild, that beyond the Mississippi lie badlands still perilled by warring Indians, that all other Americans live in penthouse apartments, drive limousine-dimension convertibles, and wear tailored furs, and that any woman without a 40-inch bust and a 20-inch waist and any man not gilded with the golden head of Adonis must not be an American. How do they know all this? They say they saw it in the movies.
>
> Going even further, many Africans regard Hollywood films as portraying an African Adam and Eve living in an American-conceived Garden of Evil. Many Hollywood films paint Africa as being only untracked jungle, ferocious tribesmen, savagery and ignorance dominating an existence of squalor by people rooted in their primitiveness. . . .
>
> The box office proves that your basic product appeals to people. Let me share with you this despatch from Latin America: "Films dealing with crime, violence, horror and sex usually give unfavorable impressions of life in the United States. However, regardless of the impressions received, movie-goers seem to enjoy American films thoroughly."

But let me be blunt about this. Films may provide a high level of audience enjoyment and at the same time convey an equally high level of negative impressions about the United States. Because audiences like the extremities of story-telling is no reason to feed them that to the exclusion of all else. Children like candy. They will eat it to excess if fed only that. But no man in his right mind would prescribe a diet of chocolate bars and ice cream. Self-restraint and control make a healthy child. I suggest that the image conveyed abroad of our land is not always a healthy one, and self-restraint may nowadays be a good prescription.

If we were to postulate, and I submit that this is true, that we are engaged in a great competition for the minds of the struggling peoples of the globe, what we present to those minds may be more than important, it may be vital. In many corners of the globe the major source of impressions about this country are the movies they meet. Would we want a future-day Gibbon or Macaulay recounting the saga of America with movies as his prime source of knowledge? Yet for much of the globe, Hollywood is just that—a prime if not sole source of knowledge. If a man totally ignorant of America were to judge our land and its civilization based on Hollywood alone, what conclusions do you think he might come to? I for one am not optimistic about the result. . . .

Come look over my shoulder again at some of the papers on my desk about the impact of Hollywood abroad.

From Thailand: a study of several thousands of the well-educated Thailand citizens—the 'elite' of that country. They had seen American pictures, and 40 percent of them believed that they were given a true picture of our country. Another 8 per cent said they thought the picture of America was 'partly true.' Do you realize this means half the educated people of that pivotal Southeast Asian country believe that the film America is the real America?

From Indonesia: 'The majority of the Indonesian population is still illiterate. . . . The masses learn of America and of our American way of life from moving pictures. They are to a large extent pictures of crime and violence, . . . pictures cruelly distorting our way of life. . . . This is a deplorable argument against us that we ourselves furnish to our Communist enemies; an argument vivid, strong, hardly forgettable.'

Forty-six visitors from 18 countries—foreign leaders brought to this country—were asked about American movies. Note this interesting figure: four out of five of them said that movies were the source of images about this country held by their countrymen and that the masses of people in their homeland *believed* what they saw.

To personalize it a bit more, sample these comments from individual foreign leaders speaking of U. S. movies in their lands:

From India: 'Movies are doing a lot of harm to America. They convey the notion that America is a country of millionaires and crooks.'

From Latin America: 'Movies are a terrible influence. . . . South Americans take the American movies seriously. They think everything they see is true.'

From Southeast Asia: 'Movies misrepresent. . . . We think of American housewives as useless drones always smoking and drinking cocktails . . .'

Murrow then closed with this note regarding censorship:

I am not here to tell you what picture to make or not to make, export or not to export. I am here mainly to suggest that you take into account another dimension not normally present in the movie-making process. That dimension is simply this: In a time when pressure is paramount and our way of life is in peril, how can I best serve my country and my people? . . .[12]

Reactions to words like these are not difficult to imagine in a community which pays men like Mr. Johnston so handsome a stipend to spread his view. Some of the flavor can be gathered in the dispatch of Murray Schumach (who was Johnny-on-the-spot at the Khrushchev caper, discussed in Chapter 4) to the *New York Times*. "Edward R. Murrow came to Hollywood last week," he wrote, "preceded by an aura of bewilderment and left a cloud of bewilderment. . . .

As far as movie men were concerned, Mr. Murrow was telling them how to run their businesses and he was giving out free advice. Movie men have heard all these criticisms many times before and they are much more keenly aware than Mr. Murrow of the problem of making movies that are both artistically and financially successful." (An odd diversion from the central theme!)

"One of Hollywood's most respected producer-directors remarked, after the meeting, that it would be a good idea if the United States Government instead of sending officials to make speeches about the importance of movies really behaved as though it believed in their importance." [13]

(It is interesting to note that, a few weeks later, film critic Bosley Crowther, who is based in New York and shows less influence by and sympathy for Hollywood producers than does reporter Shumach, took a different tack. He approved Mr. Murrow's criticisms in principle, but commented on the artistic and political difficulties in doing anything about them.) [14]

Needless to say, Mr. Johnston immediately jumped into the fray with his card catalog of testimonials, but Murrow had succeeded in dramatizing once again some ancient issues raised by the export of Hollywood films, specifically:

1. Mr. Johnston's friends notwithstanding, Hollywood movies probably do little to help America's image overseas. In fact, they may hurt it under certain circumstances or provide fuel for those biased against the United States.

2. Since we are a free society, the problem of what to do about this state of affairs short of government control of film export is a difficult one.

3. Exactly what kinds of films would have the reverse effect—or help America's cause—is anybody's guess. Crowther[15] points justifiably to the fact that certain films like "The Grapes of Wrath," "Mr. Smith Goes to Washington," and

"Citizen Kane" have displayed some of the shabbiest sides of our culture and yet have reflected best our honesty, our willingness to examine our problems, and the originality of our creative talents. Perhaps too many American films represent what is predominantly superficial and flashy in American life. What may be needed is more film drama which expresses the deep and wide aspirations of our people and the rich, heterogeneous nature of life in America.

The kinds of reproof the movies have had to suffer at the hands of critics like Murrow has rarely fallen on the printed media. The reasons are numerous. First, the press is protected by the First Amendment of our Constitution and thus possesses considerably more prestige than the movie business. Note that one is a "profession;" the other merely an industry. Second, print has traditionally been regarded as less corruptive in general than the "moving image" of films. Current distribution of *Tropic of Cancer* and *Tropic of Capricorn* in the United States, for instance, is not incommensurate with public morality in regard to sex; a film showing the same thing described by the book would not be distributed and would be regarded as corruptive. Third, print media disseminated abroad seem to attract less attention, less ballyhoo, and less razzle-dazzle than do the movies.

By no means, however, can printed media be written off as unrelated to the image of the United States overseas. But in many ways they might serve as an example to the film-makers and provide some clues as to how today's idea invaders can live up to their responsibilities.

Let us not mistake a paucity of criticism for a total absence of it. Among others, no less a man than President Kennedy has read the riot act to the gentlemen of the press for the manner in which they treated the abortive Cuban anti-Castro revolution and contributed to lowering American prestige in

foreign eyes. The press reacted as it habitually does when anyone dares criticize any of its practices—with arched back, a
feline hiss, and extended claws.

On lower levels of government, there have been others
who have had guts enough to worry aloud about the role of
the press in international affairs. Andrew H. Berding, Assistant Secretary of State for Public Affairs, on November 18,
1960, addressed a meeting of Associated Press managing
editors and voiced his concern about the problem,[16] commenting upon the tactical advantage possessed by the Soviet bloc,
for the Soviets can control their press output rigidly, while in
the United States the press is free to say what it pleases and
let government policy go hang.

"The American news agencies and those American newspapers, magazines, and news-films that circulate widely
abroad," he said, "have an ever-increasing responsibility to
give a true and balanced image of the United States to their
overseas readers and viewers. As populations increase, as literacy grows, there will be ever greater numbers of people interested in the American scene. Almost all of them will sincerely
want to understand America. They will need your help." [17]

He went on to cite various examples of what he considered
to be irresponsibility: the failure of our newspapers to put the
Little Rock incidents in the perspective of the history of race
relations in America; poor coverage of our space technology;
and lack of press sophistication in handling Soviet propaganda
statements without interpretation. In the end, Berding made a
sober plea for increased awareness on the part of editors and
publishers of their power to modify attitudes overseas.

The American press reaches everywhere in the free
world [18] and even penetrates behind the Iron Curtain. *Time*
magazine is published in the Orient, Europe and South Amer-

ica, and copies of it are even on sale at kiosks on Red Square. *Newsweek* has similar distribution. The *New York Times* is now being published in Paris, and the France-originated *Herald Tribune of Paris* has long been the most influential English-language newspaper in continental Europe. What with the *New York Times* becoming in effect a national rather than a city newspaper as of autumn, 1962,[19] its influence is almost certain to grow. *Life* magazine's bi-weekly European edition has proved immensely popular overseas. *The Reader's Digest* (which circulates thirteen million copies in the United States alone) is translated into roughly thirteen languages and sells about nine million copies abroad each month; for better or worse, it is clearly a significant contributory force in portraying America as a nation of optimistic Puritans.

Life alone circulates 745,000 copies in its Spanish and international editions. *Time* sells 615,000 copies; *Newsweek* 178,000. Not only this, but *Popular Mechanics,* which certainly speaks for America, distributes half a million copies in various foreign editions, and about sixty other American magazines—from *Oral Hygiene* in Spanish to *El automóvil americano* are exported with a combined circulation of 826,-000. Another 1,502,000 copies of American editions of over ninety other magazines, covering the wide range of interests one can see displayed at any well-stocked newsstand at home, find their ways to foreign readers.[20]

In addition to all this, American paperback books—the best and the worst of them—are beginning to flow out of the United States in great numbers. Brentano's famous bookstore in Paris, for example, has opened a paperback book club, *livre de poche américain,* and it has a mailing list of 150,-000.[21] There is considerable irony in this new prominence of paperbacks for export, since many European nations were

binding books in soft covers and selling them cheaply long before Pocket Books, Inc. began to print paperback books for
twenty-five cents in the 1930's.

The publishing industry at large has long been recognized
as an important and potentially positive organ for persuasion
favorable to the USA. Our government does not limit the export of American books, but directs their flow to libraries
and educational institutions. This move may well be an attempt at counteracting the faith that the Soviets put in printed
media to spread their ideas to others. In 1960, *forty million*
books were exported to other countries from the Soviet Union
in a variety of languages, and at least forty million more pro-
Communist volumes (such as the Cuban translation of the
works of Mao Tse-tung) were printed outside of Russia.[22]

An organization called the National Book Committee,
acutely aware of the Soviet use of the printed words, has held
a number of conferences to stimulate the sale of American
books abroad, as well as to encourage our government's Information Media Guaranty Program. The latter scheme per-
mits dollar-short buyers abroad to purchase American books
in their own currency, which Uncle Sam then uses abroad—a
neat plan for backward nations which could otherwise not afford them. The program is administered by the United States
Information Agency which itself distributes worthy books
abroad to influential citizens.[23]

In addition, the USIA has stacked its libraries with two
and a quarter million volumes, has aided in the translation
of thousands of American works into as many as fifty languages
with circulation in the millions, and has promoted the publication of seven and one-half million copies of American books
overseas. Note carefully that this has all been done not in spite
of, but with the blessing and help of the book publishing industry and their organizations, such as the American Book

Publishers' Council, the American Textbook Publishers' Institute, and others. And note also that book publishers, no doubt because their commercial interests are being served, rarely rant, rage, or tear their hair at the notion that their freedom is being abridged, the First Amendment curtailed, or the government "dictating" to them in this partnership of interests.

Consideration of this fact—and of what is regarded as one of the most successful facets of the USIA's persuasion—leads to conjecture as to why the press and the movie industry are so vulnerable to charges of damaging American prestige abroad, while the book industry appears to be serving so admirably, working *with* our government's propaganda agency, not in spite of it or against it. Possibly, if this chapter has a moral, this is where it resides. What, one might ask, differentiates the book publishing industry from journalism or the movies? Is it, perhaps, the fact that book publishers, being thoughtful folk by and large, reckon the consequences of irresponsibility in international matters as more serious a matter than do the people who publish newspapers and make films? Or is it that book publishing does not receive the colossal profits returned by other kinds of mass media, and therefore is not so avid in seeking to exploit foreign markets? Is it possible that, in fact, our government is helping the publishing industry to get business abroad, subsidizing to a degree some of their endeavors, and serving as a conduit of distribution? If the answer to any of these questions is "Yes," our government's position on the responsibility of mass communicators demands reappraisal.

There is, however, another aspect to the export and spread of American culture abroad. It is one which has lately crept onto the scene *sub rosa,* and its impact is yet to be considered. Television is fast becoming a global medium. There are some 56 million television sets in service outside the United States at the present time; by 1970 this figure could rise to 100 million with ease. There are also about 995 television stations in 82 nations beyond the borders of the United States, either on the air, under construction, planned, inactive, or experimental. (The United States has 500-odd stations.) There are 159 in the USSR; 121 in Japan; 84 in West Germany; 75 in Canada; 49 in Brazil, and 45 in the United Kingdom.[24]

Obviously, these foreign stations—in the free world, at least—are highly dependent, first, upon American methods of transmission and reception and constitute a large market for American equipment. Also, their problems in terms of programming are formidable, and here, too, they have turned to America to such an extent that 80 per cent of television fare overseas is estimated to have originated in the United States; or, put another way in the words of television critic and former producer-writer Robert Lewis Shayon, "There is hardly a foot of commercial TV film shot in the United States that is not destined, after appropriate dubbing, for the foreign re-run market." [25]

American program distributors collectively earn about $43 million in the foreign market, furnishing programs for which they may receive as much as $2,500 a half hour in Britain to as low as $105 in the Philippines. The extensive spread of American programming abroad has been going on for about four or five years in some fifty countries. There are about twenty program companies sending this material and, for the most part, they are the same organizations which produce TV fare at home—NBC, CBS, ABC, the Hollywood film-makers, the Music Corporation of America, National Telefilm Associates, and others. Some have even succeeded in making sales behind the Iron Curtain to nations like Poland and Czechoslovakia.[26]

The stuff sent abroad is exactly the same blather as we

get on our own home television receivers, with the exceptions that it must reach a low common denominator of global dimensions and a new sound track must be added for non-English speaking nations. "Sergeant Bilko," "Perry Mason," and "Como," the "Lucy" you love, "Ben Casey," Dr. Kildare," the cops, the sops, the redskins, the cowboys, the lawyers, the hoods, and the ninnies that travel through the American ether are now no longer merely American property—they belong to the world. "Bonanza," "Lassie," and "Laramie" are enjoyed as thoroughly abroad as they are at home, spokesmen for our TV industry tell us. United States TV fare has even influenced foreign programming to the degree that our who-dunits, panel parties, and Westerns are imitated by local broadcasters almost everywhere, as are our movies. It must be said, however, that something of the better goes along with the bitter, and superior programs like the "Hallmark Playhouse," the "Play of the Week," "CBS Reports," "Victory at Sea," the "NBC White Paper," and the "Project Twenty" series are also exported, but in roughly the same ratio as they appear on American television—a pretty minuscule percentage.

The result of this Americanization of television over so much of the world is disturbing to ponder, particularly since, with the successful launching of Telstar in July, 1962, one may conjecture reasonably that a world-wide television network shortly will come into being. In almost every country flooded with American telecasts, a howl has been raised by nationals concerned, first, about the rampant introduction of American values into their cultural life and, second, about the tendency of American programming to reduce employment of local artists and to stifle local initiative in developing television fare.

Reprisals against American TV have reflected this state of mind. In Canada, 55 per cent of all TV fare must be home-grown; only 14 per cent of the programs on Britain's ITA network may be foreign-originated; Japan has a relatively low ceiling on prices that may be paid for United States shows; shows for Argentina must be dubbed in Argentine dialect—not Mexican, not Castilian, and not Peruvian. All of these are restrictions which tend to limit what might otherwise be a total saturation of foreign TV programming with American products. It is almost certain that these concerns will deepen and these restrictions will increase, both where they now obtain and in nations where they are persently absent, as TV services extend in scope.

Whatever effect these programs have at present on the attitudes of millions of non-Americans is only the beginning. Television as an instrument interpreting life in the United States to other nations is likely to reduce the movies and all printed media to forces of quite minor importance.

Robert Lewis Shayon views it all with alarm.[27] He sees the challenge of global programming as one which will end up by spreading abroad primitive fare geared to common elements of taste in a world community of vastly different cultures. He considers, not unwisely, that if all we have to offer the world is our facility in the production of horse and soap operas, we are likely to lose by sheer default our hegemony of world broadcasting to the USSR, whose TV propaganda (as broadcast today in Russia) at least seems to give the viewer credit for a bit of intelligence and treats him as if he were slightly more complex than a twitchy, sexy funny bone. Should the Soviets gain the eyes and ears of the world in this manner, they doubtless would gain a considerable propaganda advantage in the cold war.

What Shayon asks for is a philosophy of broadcasting "in the public interest" blown up to global dimensions. This may not be a bad idea, but such a philosophy must relate not only to broadcasting of voices and pictures through the air. Our policy must touch *all* ideas and all purveyors of ideas beyond our shores, whether these weapons be photographed on film, stamped on newsprint, or found between the covers of a book like this one.

IT'S FUN TO BE FAT

*I recognize that many Americans have what I called the im-
perialism of efficiency. It doesn't look like imperialism. But
because the American has had more experience in certain
fields, he goes in, looks around and says, "You ought to do
it this way or you ought to do it that way." Some of these
countries have been fighting for decades, even centuries, to
get control of their own affairs, to feel like masters in their
own house. They resent being crowded or pushed too far or
too fast, although the American doesn't think he is doing
that. Then he comes home and he feels a little resentful. After
all we did for them, and they aren't appreciative!*

> —REPRESENTATIVE WALTER H. JUDD, at a special
> session of the Seventeenth Congress of the Interna-
> tional Chamber of Commerce, 1959

*Going abroad "just to do business" was once a purely per-
sonal decision for an Amercian. Today, it is one which affects
not only his own but many other nations.*

> —THOMAS AITKEN, JR.[1]

The business of America is business.

> —CALVIN COOLIDGE in a speech to the Society of
> American Newspaper Editors, January 17, 1925

ARE you aware that in 1960 the United States exported 33,-240 pounds of pickles to Saudi Arabia? Or that 14,370 pounds of prunes went to Ethiopia? That 6,632 pounds of chewing gum were shipped to Cambodia? 109,684 pounds of toilet tissue to Egypt? 16,512 pounds of aspirin to Vietnam? $46,-010 worth of hair stickum to Ghana? 129,536 sets of false teeth to Thailand? $5,663 worth of fishing rods to Uruguay? 1,329 dozen toothbrushes to Kuwait?

The above minutiae have been taken from two fascinating documents printed by the United States Department of Commerce.[2] Bound in lemon yellow cardboard, and a bargain at two dollars each, they comprise 536 pages of tiny type in three columns per page listing all our exports from sausage casings (952,980 pounds to West Germany, home of the knockwurst) to air-conditioners (one unit to Norway, fourteen to Denmark, 326 to Sweden, two to Finland, and eighty —repeat eighty—to Iceland*) in any particular year, 1960 at present perusal. In fact, over 130,000 entries in the two vol-

---

* Air conditioners are used to cool unventilated electronic equipment and supplies as well as people.

umes indicate the immensity of America's export businesses
and the spread which American-made goods achieve throughout the world today.

Add to this picture two other facets about American business influence abroad. First, American firms have many offices, agencies, salesmen, and contractors overseas, all speaking for us and our way of life. Second, American firms buy
enormous quantities of foreign-made goods through agents
overseas and constitute a formidable market, for which production is geared and which it influences directly. American
consumption dictates what is produced, how much is fabri-
cated, and what the market price for goods and labor is at any
time for many foreign industries.

The enormity of it all is not easy to grasp—nor is the extent of the influence which the business community of the
United States exerts in foreign lands. This commercial activity
cannot help but create a projection of America, affect dispositions toward the United States, and modify attitudes relating
to her in every nation which does business with her. There
are those who would even go so far as to claim that this
sphere of influence shrinks to dimensions of unimportance our
government's efforts at propaganda, the effects of our tourists
in the pleasure route, or the impact of privately produced
American books, periodicals, films, or television shows.

In the first place, American exports have been growing
lately. Since 1959, quotas restricting the sale of American
goods in foreign lands have been vanishing.[3] While American
products usually have a higher price tag than comparable
domestic items, there are evidently enough of them and in
wide enough variety to constitute a market of formidable proportions. And even though the claim is heard that we resist
tailoring our products and training our salesmen to deal with

foreign customers,[4] the record indicates that our export trade is far from insignificant.

What is even more interesting is the rate at which the export market is expanding. We are currently exporting over $20 billion worth of goods, and the rate of increase seems to be about 10 per cent per year. When Western Europe and Japan liberalized their discriminatory policies against the United States and began to expand their own economies, Uncle Sam felt the results. We have also found solid markets in some of the rapidly expanding underdeveloped nations.[5]

Of the more than $20 billion worth of goods, the pie is divided as follows: about $6 billion go to Western Europe; $194 million to Eastern Europe; $672 million to the Middle East; $2.5 billion or so to Asia (with the lion's share landing in Japan); $750 million to Africa; and the rest distributed around the world in dribbles, with the notable exception of the People's Republic of China—although it is interesting to note that Soviet Russia, in 1960 received $38 million worth of American exports as opposed to $7 million the previous year.[6] One might expect that the effect of American goods and the message they have to relay about the American way of life are directly proportional to the distribution of these exports. This, of course, is exactly the case.

Let us not forget, also, the extent of American investment abroad. Here again the pattern is one of increase. In 1950 American investment overseas was about $11.5 billion. By 1958 it was up to nearly $30 billion.[7] It is probably higher than that now. Manufacturing and the petroleum industry account for most of this vast sum, but the food industry, chemicals, transportation equipment, and other businesses have shown enormous spurts in their overseas operations over the past twelve years.[8]

Of course, quantity alone means very little, so let us see if we can penetrate the smokescreen of figures to answer the fundamental question which puzzles the observer. What effect does American business have, not upon the world market, but upon the attitudes of foreigners toward that giant industrial nation, the United States, whose technological genius and consumer goods are being exported almost everywhere?

The effects have been noticeable. Perhaps one of the most important areas where the influence of America has been felt is in mother's shopping bag. All over Western Europe and in Great Britain large American-style supermarkets have been multiplying like rabbits, many of them using American equipment and financed in part with American capital.[9] Boasting check-out counters, self-service, and wide ranges of consumer goods like their American counterparts, these merchandising palaces have captured the fancy of the European housewife with their conveniences and—most important—generally lower price tags than those in conventional retail stores.

La méthode américaine, as the French call the American way of food marketing, has unquestionably aroused the ire of the old style *boucher, boulanger,* and *épicier,* but its success speaks for itself. Wherever it goes, the supermarket idea can be modified to accord with local customs—for example, by expanding the *pasta* counter in Naples, or introducing frozen foods gingerly and tactfully to housewives who still prefer to shell peas or wash Brussels sprouts.

Other straws in the wind indicate pretty clearly that *la méthode américaine* will not stop its modification of European life with the supermarkets. "Snack bars" have been creeping onto the scene since World War II. Some of the slickest have long been operating in Rome, Milan, London, and other large cities. But now even the French, long the last-ditch defenders of the leisurely continental lunch *avec* wine, good talk, and a period of post-digestive contemplation, are beginning to adopt the American idea of the quick lunch.[10] Grocery stores are sprouting snack counters. Parisians line up for sandwiches, a hamburger, or that classic comestible which made the trip from Germany to France via the United States, *le hot dog*— usually pronunced "dug" in Paris, but the real item nonetheless. *Avec le Coke,* it's mighty tasty, and plans are in the works for a chain of roadside restaurants which will feature quick service and "one place meals." Next stop: *Le drive-in avec l' hôtesse attirant.*

The distribution of other kinds of American consumer ideas—American-made consumer goods themselves—have come in for more criticism than the export of the supermarket or lunch counter. At the time of the United States Trade Fair in Great Britain, *Business Week* published[11] a number of criticisms of United States export policy which may summarize European attitudes.

First, it was observed that we frequently sell leftovers to the foreign market, things that we cannot sell at home. Second, the charge was heard that American goods are rarely adapted for the foreign market; American electrical goods for instance, which are needed in Europe and elsewhere, are not modified for European voltages. Third, it was noted that many American firms seemed to expect greater profits from overseas sales than from domestic markets, quite the reverse of the trade preference which foreign countries, in their eagerness for dollars, have given the United States. Fourth, a number of American business men, according to Europeans, seem shifty about quoting prices, preferring to state their prices in terms of the United States market without clarifying what insurance and freight charges overseas are likely to be. *Business Week* states, however, that American products are warmly received where there are no local equivalents. In this regard, it is interesting to note that West Germany has cold-shouldered many American "gadgets" in favor of superior local fabrications, in spite of which Detroit now pins great hopes on the possibility of at least commanding the foreign market with their line of "compact" cars, clearly imitations of the postwar European economy vehicles.[12]

Other kinds of problems emerge for American business abroad. Paul Zucker, the public relations expert, cites[13] the case of an American dishwasher concern that ran into trouble because the ease and convenience of the dishwasher did not impress the Swiss housewife to whom it was being sold. The Swiss, an industrious people, could not understand how anyone would want to turn over to a machine the pleasure of washing dishes. There is some concern, too, about local limitations which are placed on the advertising of American commodities in countries like Argentina, Great Britain, and Belgium, thereby making it difficult for American consumer goods to create the kinds of impressions on their customers that they make in the United States.[14]

Objections to American business overseas have also been raised here at home,[15] mostly by partisan organizations with axes to grind. Labor union interests resent the fact that European workmen are presently making components for American automobiles, typewriters, and sewing machines, as well as recording music for the sound tracks of American television programs at wages a good deal below those earned by their American counterparts. Such sniping cannot help but be noted eventually overseas and create hostility in nations where certain kinds of labor can be performed as expertly as in the United States, and far more economically. Labor's attitude, in this respect (while unquestionably well-intended), is likely to be regarded as the most rabid kind of nationalism when viewed from abroad.

Strange as it may seem, one nation which shows signs of being considerably impressed with American technology and consumer goods is the USSR. American-style consumer goods appear to be the rage there, much to the puzzlement of Soviet officials, since almost no decadent, Western luxuries are imported into Russia. Harrison E. Salisbury, expert on Soviet affairs and a one-time Moscow correspondent, has written, "Nothing infuriates party propagandists more than the blue-jean fad. They declare that this is a completely alien style. They note that blue denim material is not even produced in the Soviet Union. Where the blue jeans come from is not certain. But it is believed they are smuggled in from Berlin through Poland." [16]

These blue jeans, along with a preoccupation by the Soviet teenagers with American dances, fashions, and vocabulary, provide a good indication of just how far—for better or worse —the American style of life has traveled and how difficult it is to keep it out once foreigners get a whiff of our way of doing things.

In addition to jazz and blue jeans, Communist Russia seems to be copying another American business custom: the advertising of consumer goods.[17] As long as state-produced items were in short supply, there was, of course, no necessity for Soviet distributors and manufacturers to tout their wares *à la* USA. With surpluses of certain items on hand, Soviet officials have taken a leaf or two from Madison Avenue's copybook and have begun buying space in newspapers, using "spot" commercials on television and radio, and plastering notices of goods for sale on the ubiquitous billboards which heretofore had been largely reserved for morale-building and ideological messages. Soviet ads, by the way, tend to be conservative, solemn, and understated.

Just about the best serious discussion of the over-all psychological effects of American exports and industry abroad is found in a small but powerful book by Thomas Aitken, Jr., an advertising man with considerable experience in the field of international trade—from whom the short quotation at the beginning of this chapter was taken. Entitled *A Foreign Policy For American Business,* Aitken's book emphasizes particularly the obligations that American business men have overseas as unofficial but potent representatives of American policy and as agents of diplomacy.

In the witty opening chapter,[18] Aitken postulates a mythical economic invasion of America. He tells the story of an Italian motor scooter factory that decides to locate in Midtown, USA. He examines the discontents of the American natives when the Italians violate local taboos, step on local customs, create jealousies and rivalries in their effort, as the Italian purchasing manager puts it, "just to do business." At the end of the chapter, it is clear that no industry can move into a foreign nation "just to do business," any more than products can be exported overseas without creating a psychological impression upon the people who use them. The by-product of business in these instances is propaganda, good or bad, for the nations involved in the transaction, and modification in one degree or another of attitudes and opinions within them.

Aitken goes on to examine the background of American foreign trade, outlining the story of the nineteenth-century American individualist who makes his "killing" overseas. He indicates that some companies do not take their activities abroad seriously, sending second-rate men to staff their foreign offices, hiring local labor at rates far below what they pay Americans (but above local scale), and upsetting local economics by paying wages that are above local standards. Some businesses merely use foreign branches as window dressing for prestige. Often American employees overseas are clannish, disrespectful of local customs, ignorant of the local language, boorish and superior.

"American businessmen abroad," observes Aitken, "having assumed a responsibility for our country's image overseas, should not leave this vital area of personal contact to our embassy or consulate alone. . . ." [19] In summary, he provides an eight-point series of statements which stand as a commonsense set of guidelines for all Americans who are concerned with overseas commerce on the one hand, and with the image of their nation in the minds of non-Americans on the other. They are:

1. American business is a facet of American foreign policy.
2. With reasonable support from its own government, American business will face the risks of helping with development of emerging countries, and it is prepared also to forward this policy in cooperation with the business interests of our Western allies and Japan.
3. American investment abroad should, to the extent possible, represent the principle of public corporate ownership in the area in which it operates.
4. Basic personnel policies should be the same as in the United States, allowing foreign employees equal opportunities. Adaptations to local employer-employee relationships are necessary.
5. The business and its American personnel should become part of the local community.
6. In order to interpret fairly the American principles it represents, the business should give special care to the use of expert advice and techniques in communicating with the foreign public and its components.
7. Because its mainsprings and aspirations are identical with our nation as represented by American embassies and other government agencies abroad, it should maintain an open channel of communications with them.

And, finally, a provision which warrants separate discussion and support, one to which all the foregoing issues have pointed:

8. American business must insist that American government become aware of the international responsibility that business now bears and so give full consideration to the conditions necessary to the fulfillment of its social, as well as its commercial, objectives.[20]

A sounder set of principles would be difficult to articulate. What is disturbing, however, is the inference derived from Aitken's deep concern as to the degree to which American business overseas has not lived up to them in the years since World War II, and the probable ensuing damage, which may well be impossible to undo. This may be of less moment in Western Europe, where our allies are firmly behind us, but quite worrisome in South America, where American industry —particularly the petroleum industry—has vast interests upon which we in the United States are highly dependent. In Latin America our image leaves much to be desired, as the reception given former Vice-President Nixon there a few years ago indicates. The corporate behavior of American firms and the attitudes of American business men have not done much to ameliorate the situation there. As this hostility to American business grows, so does the power of the Latin American Communist parties. Communist Cuba as a neighboring country is as nothing when compared to the possibility of a Communist (or near-Communist) *continent* to the south.[21]

It is worth noting, however, that some American businesses are keenly aware of this problem and are, in fact, leaning over backward to avoid rubbing Latin American fur the wrong way while working to reduce the image of the United States as an imperialistic power. Robert L. Heilbroner has observed[22] that the Standard Oil Company, for instance, after its unfortunate experiences in the past in Mexico, is today handling its Venezuelan interests with kid gloves. The company is presently paying the highest local wages in the country, turning half its local profits back to Venezuela and even training local administrators to take control of the company some day when the American parent organization steps out of the country.

Another significant force in spreading abroad the most attractive side of American business is our representation at various trade fairs around the world.[23] The sign of our successes at these fairs is the fact that in a number of cases we have even frightened Soviet exhibitors away, since they are reluctant to take second place to such fascinating exhibits as *Cinerama* movies and re-creations of American homes.

Hundreds of these fairs are held yearly around the world, both behind the Iron Curtain and in front of it in such diverse countries as Cyprus, Nigeria, and Vietnam. Most of them take place in relatively developed countries, however, and the United States does well at them because it has the most fully developed economy in the world and can display the most impressive goods and products.

It was not until 1954 that President Eisenhower, concerned that America was not officially represented at many of these functions, appropriated $2,250,000 in order that the Department of Commerce and the United States Information Agency might recruit a staff of architects, designers, and idea men to make sure that our overseas exhibits would show our best features in a context meaningful to foreign eyes. So we talked agriculture to the Italians, fruit-farming to the Spaniards, and jute production to the Pakistani with generally good results. Not only was (and is) much trade stimulated by these fairs, but they constitute healthy propaganda. Especially do they drive their message home by utilizing a trade mission usually composed of six members—a panel of experts from government and industry who answer questions about American products and exports as honestly and directly as they can.[24]

What all this spread of American culture means is that, externally at least, more and more people around the world are becoming more and more like Americans in terms of the material aspects of life. Edwin L. Dale, writing in Paris, discusses this new affluence as follows:

> Materially, the West European is changing fast, and will change more. Many aspects of his life reflect the change. Inexorably, the statistics march on: car registrations, telephone saturation, number of self-service stores and supermarkets, television ownership, number of household appliances. Home ownership statistics are sketchy, but the evidence of one's eyes and ears is that home ownership is increasing, too (in some countries, like Italy, primarily in the form of ownership of flats or apartments). The evidence is overwhelming that the European of whatever country, regardless of vastly different habits and traditions is, as susceptible as the American to the lure of things material, from washing machines to variety in clothing. The advertising business is booming. And thus, from the point of view of what he has and how he lives, the Western European is already becoming increasingly like the American.[25]

But is this affluence really "Americanizing" non-Americans? Dale doubts it, suggesting that these material symptoms of change are ends in themselves, not means to fundamental cultural changes. The average European, he suggests, does not find that his basic attitudes and feelings about the important things in life—love, education, or politics, for instance—are becoming "Americanized" just because he suffers traffic jams, owns a television set, and has acquired a taste for catsup. Implicit in Dale's argument is the assumption, therefore, that this export of American material culture is a negligible factor in terms of our image overseas.

Dale may have a valid point, but one wonders if he does not oversimplify a complex situation. It is too soon to tell what the effect of America's economic (and, as a by-product, cultural) influence on the rest of the world will be in the long run. Dale notwithstanding, material changes seem to bring psychological changes along with them, as those of us who have eaten a steak dinner after a week of K rations, or who have moved to a spacious house from a one-room hovel, can testify. Whether the psychological changes that accompany the affluence we export will produce, as a by-product, a better image of America and a disposition to place faith in our nuclear, foreign and military policies, is anybody's guess. But it is reasonable to assume that friendly attitudes follow one another even if they relate to different kinds of issues—up to a point. Where the point is, and what history will have to say about how far our allies and the neutral nations allowed their acceptance of American material goods and business expertise to color other essentially irrelevant attitudes, had best be left to the necromancers.

There is another side to this problem also, and it is one that is frequently forgotten in discussions concerning how we export the American "way of life." This is the simple fact that the USSR has entered the international export market in terms of manufactured goods, natural resources, and investments, and she has one very important advantage on her side.[26] In a government-controlled economy, the state can afford to absorb international business losses by charging them off to domestic financial surpluses in a manner that would be literal suicide for private enterprise. In competition for foreign markets, therefore, Russia can undercut the competition financially, and it is this fact that lies in the background of Nikita Khrushchev's claim that he will "bury" the capitalist nations.

At present, exports from the entire Soviet bloc make up

about half of what the USA exports—one-third of those of free Europe.[27] But the Russians are hell-bent to catch up with the USA in this area as well as improving their own internal economy. One practice of the Soviets is to buy vast quantities of raw materials and "dump" them into the world market at low prices, thus upsetting the natural market value. Another Soviet trick is to buy huge quantities or total outputs of various industries from nations like Burma or Egypt for abnormally high prices and use this procedure as a political lever abroad to insure the election of leftist governments. This stunt worked in Finland where the Soviet Union, by cancelling a mammoth order for ships, caused enough unemployment to unseat a government hostile to the USSR.

Russian foreign investments are trifling compared to those of the USA—about 1/25th of ours. But the Soviets get a lot of mileage out of very little. Most of our investment finds its way to relatively prosperous nations where it is indeed noticed, but where it does not make a crucial difference in terms of national prosperity. A mere 10 per cent goes to poor countries. The USSR, on the other hand, invests almost exclusively in "have-not" nations such as India, Egypt, Syria, Yemen, Afghanistan, and Indonesia, where Soviet engineers build much needed factories, irrigation systems, dams, and other highly conspicuous technological projects which have considerable propaganda value. Also, the Soviet Union does not—unlike private free world corporations—need to think of profits from foreign investments. They constitute, in fact, a form of foreign aid to neutral and underdeveloped nations which are paid for by the expanding and increasingly prosperous Soviet economy.

To counter both of these kinds of competition, many suggestions have been made. Obviously, private industry cannot compete with Soviet exports if the Russians are going to play havoc with the stability of the market. Private industry should be, and is, given relief and appropriate loans by the free-world governments. Lowering of tariff barriers—a recent trend —is another solution. Also, it is most essential to neutralize the powerful propaganda which the Soviet Union, by means of conspicuous good works and good words, has employed in underdeveloped countries. Foreign aid and the stimulation of foreign investments in these countries by means of loans and tax preferences are the weapons which can accomplish this. From a political point of view, the vital question may well be whether our enormous affluence is being directed to the right places around the world, that is, to the places where it is needed to combat anti-Americanism and hostility to our international policies vis-à-vis the USSR.

Most notably our government's International Cooperation Agency coordinates the various agencies administrating foreign aid, stressing and encouraging material aid to those "have-not" nations which need it most and technical assistance to those countries which require it as they industrialize or expand their economies. This assistance is paid for either in part or entirely by the country requesting assistance or by an overseas relief agency here in the United States.[28] The relationship of the ICA to American private enterprise is, of course, marginal, but in a sense this organization mediates between our gigantic surplus-producing economy and those countries which can use the materials and technical know-how we can spare.

Another similar project on which our government has embarked gives special economic relief to those nations which need it most, and is designed to direct our enormous agricultural surplus overseas to nations whose foodstuff supplies are short. It is President Kennedy's Food For Peace program which allows foreign nations to purchase American agricultural products—but only agricultural products *in their own*

currency, not in United States dollars (one of the most stable
currencies in the world) as heretofore. Dollar shortages have
prevented these countries in the past from using any of our
surpluses, unless they happened to receive them as gifts re-
sulting from one or another of our foreign aid programs.[29]

President Kennedy's Alliance for Progress is a similar
scheme, but directed to Latin America as a hedge against any
further tendencies in that corner of the globe to thumb the
nose at Uncle Sam by embracing Communism.[30] Under Ad-
ministrator Teodoro Moscoso, the Alliance, during its first
year, earmarked $1,029,576,000 in loans and grants to South
American nations for improvement in many areas. In addition, President Kennedy has requested that rich Latin Americans contribute their share to local bootstrap operations as the
best defense against Communist expansion in our hemisphere.
It probably is.

Writing about the Alliance for Progress, The *New York
Times* has said:

> The Alliance for Progress is more than the answer to the
> Cuban revolution. It is an attempted answer to one of the most
> momentous and menacing problems of our times, which is how
> the economically underdeveloped areas of the world can meet
> the insistent popular demands for social justice and economic
> development. The Communist method is revolution followed
> by totalitarian government. We say the goals can better be
> reached by our evolutionary, democratic, capitalistic and free
> enterprise system.
>
> President Kennedy has shrewdly pointed out that to prove
> this is "our unfulfilled task." Statesmen, economists and sociol-
> ogists have for years been arguing, that the few rich nations
> (the United States and Canada, Western Europe, Australia
> and New Zealand) are getting richer, while the underdeveloped
> world—perhaps as much as three-quarters of the non-Commu-
> nist world—is getting poorer.
>
> The Alliance for Progress is a brave effort to prove that

one of the major underdeveloped areas of the world can be launched on an upward spiral if Latin Americans will make the social and economic reforms that are necessary and if we help with long-range financial aid and technical advice. A great deal is at stake in the Alliance for Progress. Every government, every statesman, politician, businessman, landowner and intellectual in the Western Hemisphere should be working to make it a success.[31]

Such moves on the part of our government indicate clearly one main fact: it is unwise, considering Soviet competition and the importance of America's economic influence abroad, to leave this matter entirely or perhaps even largely in private hands. While a capitalist economy seems capable of flourishing as a self-contained unit or in competition with other capitalist economies, it faces different problems in international competition with communism. First, in terms of competing for foreign markets and in investments overseas, a Communist country is not necessarily impelled by the profit motive—if it is relatively affluent. This is exactly what the USSR may be rapidly becoming. It can *afford* to compete on all levels with American capitalism and sustain losses to win out in the end. Second, a Communist nation, free from the need to make money in foreign trade, can use its international economic policy to achieve the greatest number of propaganda advantages it can receive per dollar—or ruble; in other words, it can invest where investments are needed, not where they are necessarily profitable. Private enterprise, on the other hand, must do business which will produce a margin of profit, and therefore it will invest where the chances of financial successes are highest. This will not automatically accrue to the propaganda advantage of capitalistic nations.

There is only one solution to this problem, and it is the one that the United States, albeit reluctantly, has accepted as necessary. It is a realistic and cooperative effort to be shared by business, investment, and government. Private enterprise has to be permitted a wide margin of opportunity to invest overseas and export American goods to other countries. And the American taxpayer, via his government, will have to supplement the efforts of private enterprise by means of tariff arrangements, loans, gifts, and fiscal policies in those areas of the world where private enterprise finds it burdensome to operate. By duplicating the advantage that the USSR has over the free world, that is, by dipping into our internal national wealth via taxation, we will be able to meet Russian competition both on the economic and on the propaganda level. It is unfortunate, of course, that the only way to offset the wiles of Russian policy is to be equally wily ourselves, but this is a strategic principle of persuasion which many a propagandist has had to learn the hard way in the bitter crucible of failure.

America's business genius, technology, and wealth of consumer goods that her capitalist system has made available to so many of her citizens are the objects of admiration and envy around the world. Envy, however, rarely leads to amity. During one's travels one can hardly help feeling that the reason for the disparagement of and hostility toward America is the proverbial green-eyed monster of jealousy working on an international scale.

For this, if not for other reasons, we must face one harsh reality of the second half of the twentieth century. This cannot be an American Century as it was described in the popular press for a few years after World War II. It must be, instead, a century of common sharing by the free nations—and perhaps the Communist nations as well—of the technology, raw materials, advertising inventiveness and abundance of consumer goods that is presently possible even for the nations which have been undeveloped until now.

That the United States has led the way is a sheer accident

of fate, attendant on our vast national resources (which were largely untapped until about the nineteenth century), the heterogeneity of the immigrants who came to our shores, and the fact that we have been spared the devastation of modern warfare on our territory for one hundred years. There is nothing mystical, "right," or essentially sacred about our hegemony in the world of commerce.

Perhaps one blueprint for what the future holds in store for the free world lies in the model of the European Common Market. Here, petty differences in ways of doing business, obsolete tariff restrictions, and outworn fears of government intervention into private business have given way to a realistic pooling of resources to break down nationalistic barriers, which in the past prevented the continent as a whole from utilizing fully each country's special economic strength. Some observers go so far as to predict that the Common Market may provide the psychological climate for the eventual establishment of a United States of Europe. If anything can do it, mutual economic interdependence can.

Let us look, however, beyond the European Common Market to the possibilities of a Free World Common Market, an alliance of all the capitalist and quasi-Socialist lands (like Sweden), the object of which would be to raise to a decent level the economic status of *all* the free nations and to introduce primitive and backward areas of the world to the good life which only a handful of countries have thus far achieved. Again, such an alliance would have psychological concomitants of profound importance in uniting the free world in spirit and in fact.

We are, of course, moving in this direction, but two observations are in order. First, we are not moving fast enough, considering the rate of Soviet expansion and increases in overseas trade. Second, any ideas that America will control, administer, or direct this Common Market, or that such trade practices must affirm American economic leadership in the world, or that they may become an excuse for America's economic control of other countries must be scotched before they start. To put it bluntly, such notions would be the worst kind of international propaganda for our side.

PART THREE

AMERICA SPEAKS

COMES THE REVOLUTION!

We do not claim perfection in our own society and in our own lives, but we do maintain that the direction we take is always that of greater liberty.

We believe that justice, decency and liberty, in an orderly society, are concepts which have raised man above the beasts of the field. To deny any person the opportunity to live under their shelter is an offense against all humanity.

Our republic is the product of the first successful revolution against colonialism in modern times. Our people, drawn from all nations of the world, have come to these shores in the search for freedom and opportunity in a progressive society. We have never forgotten either our origins or the nature of the world we live in.

And that is why we Americans do not fear the winds of change and the winds of freedom which are blowing across so much of the world. To us, they make a wonderful sound; and as the seeds of which they carry take root and grow, we will feel that America's great purpose in this role is being fulfilled.

—ADLAI E. STEVENSON, United States Ambassador to the United Nations in a TV address, January 3, 1962

The continuing tragedy in our country is the failure to realize that propaganda is a weapon in many ways far more powerful than conventional or even nuclear weapons . . . Propaganda has become an ultimate weapon, a substitute for war, a painless death whereby one by one the limbs and organs of a free society are narcotized or excised.

—STUART HANNON of Radio Free Europe, in an address at Notre Dame University, November 20, 1961

I believe that we have no more important job than to insure that the people of all countries receive the truth so that they will be able to reach intelligent judgments.

—PRESIDENT JOHN F. KENNEDY in a letter to Radio Free Europe

AMERICANS are notorious for their social zeal both at home and abroad. And where there is opportunity there is considerable effort on the part of private interests to participate in the public affairs of the nation. The cold war is one focal point for this kind of missionary involvement on the part of those who do not want to stand idly by while the Soviet Union gobbles up neighboring countries and clamps the lid upon the free interchange of ideas within its own territory. Incensed by the iniquities and abuses that they have seen in the Soviet bloc countries, various private citizens have decided to do something about them. Whether they have been in the main successful remains a moot point.

Of course every effort of this kind, as we have seen in the preceding chapters, requires that those Americans who make contact with people overseas recognize that they are assuming a major responsibility for the welfare of Uncle Sam and his international interests and diplomatic policies. Such contacts are —or may become—matters of life or death whenever they lead to misunderstanding and confusion or blur the goals of American policy in the delicate relationships which the United States maintains with her adversaries in the cold war. The price of freedom to do something as private citizens about the tyrannies under which Iron Curtain countries exist is responsibility to the goals and objectives of the free societies of the world.

Responsibility is the central problem, it seems to us, of the two major private organizations which probe behind the Iron Curtain and represent the political and diplomatic interests of the USA: Radio Free Europe and Radio Liberty. Both are, as we shall show, similar in nature and objectives. And yet they are separate organizations, the former broadcasting only to satellite nations, the latter only to the Soviet Union. And each organization must face a vastly different challenge and play a distinct variation on the same theme in the cold war of words. In spite of these differential factors, however, both pose for us the vital question, "Comes the revolution—then what?" Does the USA really want the revolution in the first place?

Radio Free Europe is the older (by three years) of the two, and so it will be dealt with first.[1] It is actually one of the five divisions of a parent organization, the Free Europe Committee, which was born, in theory at least, back in 1949. The Committee grew out of a number of conversations between such high-level Americans as foreign policy expert George Kennan, ex-Ambassador Joseph C. Grew, and his one-time colleague, De Witt C. Poole. Joined by others of equal stature (including a retired general named Eisenhower), they conceived their basic aim: to provide for the free world an outlet for the ideas and voices of exiled nationals in the nations which had recently fallen to Soviet imperialism in East Europe, namely, Czechoslovakia, Hungary, Poland, Rumania, and Bulgaria.

RFE's early years and growing pains are more or less irrelevant here, but the Committee managed to receive initial financing (it is not exactly clear how and from whom) and has been a potent force on the international scene ever since. At present, it is supported partially by the public through contributions stimulated by the Advertising Council's donated services as fund-raisers, the sweat of volunteer workers, and some seventy national organizations such as the Boy Scouts, Kiwanis International, the American Legion, and many others of different stripes and persuasions.[2]

As to whether these contributions actually pay most of the bills for the massive enterprise, the Crusade for Freedom, remains anyone's guess. The Free Europe Committee has never opened its books to public scrutiny. According to a spokesman for the organization, its financing comes strictly from the United States—meaning that it does not represent the financial resources of the deposed (and mostly capitalistic) governments of the satellite nations.

The present president of the Free Europe Committee is John Richardson, Jr., a prominent lawyer and investment banker, Harvard man, ex-Army officer, and director and member of the boards representing any number of worthy causes. On May 1, 1961, he left the investment banking firm of Paine, Webber, Jackson and Curtis to head the Committee. Richardson is a church deacon and has shown his sympathy for the plight of the captive peoples by adopting a young escapee from the Hungarian uprising of 1956, a revolution which, as we shall see, gave RFE its share of headaches.[3]

The Free Europe Committee has five operating arms at present, although RFE is undoubtedly the most familiar to the public.[4] First, there is the Communist Bloc Operations, which publishes an excellent monthly magazine called *East Europe,* a periodical review of the affairs of East European countries from the point of view of exiles from these nations; it is distributed within the United States and Western Europe in the languages of the satellite nations and in English. Free World Operations assists organizations such as Freedom House and various foreign policy groups by making available to them research materials and the services of experts on Eastern Europe. Its Exile Political Organizations maintains liaison with exiles and exile groups from satellite nations, while West European Operations, with its headquarters in London, offers "assistance" to people involved in West European affairs.

The above phrasing describing the functions of these four divisions is largely that of the Free Europe Committee itself. Except for the publication of *East Europe,* the Committee keeps relatively mum about what these divisions actually do in terms of "assistance," "research," and other projects vaguely but frequently mentioned in connection with the Free Europe Committee and the Committee for Liberation. (More of the latter in a subsequent discussion.)

Finally we return to Radio Free Europe, and about *its* nature there is little secret. In 1961 its headquarters were transferred from New York to Munich in order to keep its fingers more firmly on the pulse of the international scene. Some 85 per cent of its programs originate in its studios there. RFE employs some 1,600 persons, about 1,100 of them stationed in Munich, 100 in New York, and 400 in Portugal, where it operates a relay site for its programs.

The top management of RFE is made up of Americans, but the programs are written and broadcast by Eastern European nationals. While more than half the Munich staff are East Europeans, policy in general is dictated by Americans, in which regard it is understood that RFE has the unofficial blessing of our State Department.

At present, RFE's policy is largely formulated in Munich. (Before 1961 this task was done in New York and directives were transmitted daily to Munich.) In Munich also the Research and Evaluation Department studies Soviet bloc publications, monitors broadcasts behind the Iron Curtain from about fifty stations, and interviews refugees from satellite nations in order to provide data upon which those entrusted with both policy and programming can act.

RFE employs twenty-eight powerful transmitters for its broadcasts in six languages—Czech, Slovak, Hungarian, Polish, Rumanian, and Bulgarian. Several transmitters are often used at the same time for the same broadcast to minimize jamming, and the service is on the air around the clock for almost 3,000 hours a week, making it just about the most active broadcasting system in the free world—probably busier than either the British Broadcasting Company's combined foreign and domestic services or the Voice of America.

RFE's propaganda policy is difficult to pinpoint,[5] and that is perhaps as it should be in a world as mercurial as the one in which we are living. Briefly stated, its main objective in persuasion seems to be to undo the lies and distortions commonly used by Soviet propaganda in its attempt to sell dialectical materialism and the Communist version of history.

RFE's *Annual Report* for 1961 states: "While thwarting these efforts [attempts by the USSR to cover up rifts in the Sino-Soviet alliance and to characterize the Western nations as war-mongers], Radio Free Europe marshalled its resources to help its listeners in East Europe understand the dangers to them of the unrest and ferment in the Communist world; and also to reinforce the image of Western dedication to principles of freedom, justice, human dignity and progress." [6] The report goes on to single out such incidents as Khrushchev's conflicts with the Albanian Communists, passed over in silence by the satellite press, but broadcast by RFE to the captive nations. It also concerns itself with the internal affairs of the satellite nations themselves and draws for its listeners a picture of the West as free, prosperous, and peace-seeking, in stark contrast to what they hear at home on their local radio stations.

In effect, RFE offers local radio programs to each of the five nations to which it broadcasts, except, of course, that it is free from adherence to the party lines which local broadcasters must follow. It seeks "to provide listeners behind the Iron Curtain with a complete radio service—ten minutes of the latest news, every hour on the hour, is the backbone of RFE's program schedule. In addition to news of America and the free world, RFE reports the facts about events within the listeners' own country and the Soviet bloc—facts that the Communists suppress or distort." [7]

Generally, news broadcasts seem to account for roughly one-third of RFE's program output.[8] Less than one-fifth of its air time is concerned with political commentary such as discussions of the problems of the workers in Communistic states, ideological issues in regard to Communist theory, the role of farmers in collective states, de-Stalinization in Russia, Socialism in Western Europe, political opinions of Western journalists, and similar matters. The remainder of RFE's program service is made up of non-political programs of interest to satellite nations. It may broadcast religious services, cover sports events and symphony concerts, offer entertainment and comedy, or be concerned with serious cultural fare. In general, the programs seem to be directed to intellectuals, farmers, workers, women, young people, soldiers, and civil servants, if one can judge, for instance, from the weekly log of the Voice of Free Czechoslovakia and if one wants to identify "target" audiences in terms of the community of interests to which the programs seem to point.

The young audience apparently is attracted to American jazz, and both popular and classical music is the favorite fare on RFE. But drama, satire, special events, and eye-witness coverage of many kinds are also broadcast by RFE in its enormous output. Naturally, almost all the programs are performed by émigré nationals.

Calculating RFE's effectiveness—like calculating the effectiveness of any persuasion—is far from simple. The Audience Research Department produced thirty-two surveys in 1961 which are thoroughly documented but rather dull to read. They seek to apply statistical specificity to socio-psychological factors within the satellite countries, attitudes toward the West and toward Radio Free Europe, and listeners' opinions on their own governments, communism, and the Russians.

Such studies cannot be taken at face value, however, nor can we safely conclude that RFE is having a salubrious effect in the satellite nations. The reports are based upon small samples consisting of interviews with refugees and visitors to the West who can hardly be typical of the great majority who do not defect or travel outside the Iron Curtain. Although 2,500 such interviews were held in 1961, the people conducting these surveys are intelligent enough to slide plenty of caveats into them lest they be taken as gospel or semi-gospel. They do represent, however, the best that RFE can do at present to gauge the effectiveness of its radio work, since it is doubtful that any Western door-to-door interviewers would be welcome where RFE penetrates via the airwaves.

Boiled down, the studies, as reported by RFE, indicate that RFE's efforts are by no means in vain and that a definite impression is being made by the broadcasts. Here are some major comments heard by RFE researchers in these interviews:

1. RFE provides news and information which cannot be obtained from Communist sources.

2. RFE informs captive peoples of news suppressed or distorted by Communist media.

3. Political programs on RFE are factual rather than polemical, and are helpful to the listeners in understanding internal and external events.

4. RFE provides a link with the outside world, thus reducing the isolation the Communists have imposed on their victims.

5. Communists themselves want to hear facts withheld by the party.

6. RFE sometimes inhibits Communist terror tactics as a result of intensive reportage by RFE.

7. RFE is a moral and ideological force in sustaining resistance to Communist pressures.

8. The people in satellite nations find RFE a source of hope.[9]

The respondents, as would be expected, had nearly all listened to RFE, and reported that, despite official discouragement of the practice of tuning in on foreign broadcasts, a large part of the audience, served by the more than twelve million radio sets in the five satellite countries, regularly listens to RFE programs. As an additional means of communication, much of what RFE broadcasts is relayed from individual to individual by word-of-mouth "bush telegraph." Many respondents thought that RFE is the most influential Western station in operation today and that it is probably responsible for an increase of anti-Communism behind the Iron Curtain.

One indication that RFE's claims may not be moonshine is the ferocity of the Communist attempt to jam the broadcasts —that is, to broadcast static or noise on the same frequency RFE is using and thus make reception difficult. RFE estimates that 2,500 transmitters in the satellite countries, as well as in the USSR and East Germany, are at work drowning out Western broadcasts—and a good share of them are aimed at RFE. Using various electronic devices to overcome the jamming, RFE claims that some 90 per cent of its broadcasts can be heard on at least one frequency in the captive countries despite the ubiquity of the jamming transmitters.

Another straw in the wind supporting RFE's position is the virulence of the attacks that have been leveled on it by the Communist press at home and abroad. Called rumor-mongers, liars, spies, subversives, counter-revolutionists, killers, adventurers, bloodletters, opportunists, and a host of other epithets which would hardly be forthcoming did RFE not infuriate the powers that be behind the Iron Curtain, the organization takes pride in the intensity of this onslaught and views it as a sign of success.[10] But this vilification may also be indicative of the sensitivity of the Communists to outside criticism.

RFE, on the other hand, is pretty sensitive itself, particularly in regard to the role it played in the Hungarian revolution of 1956. Volumes of literature have emerged from the Free Europe Committee and its supporters attempting to clarify RFE's part in the ill-fated attempt to overthrow the Communist masters of Hungary. The main charges against it can be summed up in the following report in an American newspaper dated December 27, 1956, after the failure of the insurrection:

RADIO FREE EUROPE IS PUT IN DOGHOUSE OVER HUNGARY

Munich, Bavaria.—Radio Free Europe, quasi-official and American-supported broadcast program, is in the European doghouse. It would be hard to find an informed German, Austrian, or Hungarian who does not believe that RFE used double-talk and veiled braggadocio to incite the Hungarians to rebellion. Worse, RFE put itself in the position of fomenting a fight with no real intention either to support it or join it. This is equivalent to the legendary boxer's manager who savagely yelled from ringside: "Fight him, Butch. He can't hurt us." [11]

In point of fact, no one will ever know how justified these charges are, so complex were the events involved in the episode, but RFE was unquestionably an important factor. James Michener's novel, *The Bridge at Andau,* contains a character, Ferenc Kobal, who expresses the disillusionment and destroyed hopes of those Hungarians who believed that America had committed itself in free-world broadcasts to come to the aid of the rebels. Kobal states:

Do you know why Hungarians like me are so bitter against the United States? For six years you fed us this propaganda. For six years the Russians trampled us in the mud. But when we rose in rebellion for the very things you told us to fight for, how many Americans stepped forth to help us? Not one. Who did join our side? Russian troops. How many American tanks helped us? Not one. What tanks did join us in our fight for freedom? Russian tanks. This is a terrible indictment.[12]

RFE's part in the Hungarian fiasco (as well as in the Poznan riots and other Polish incidents) has been investigated in the free world *ad nauseam*. The International Research Associates, Inc.[13] interviewed refugees, the Bonn government reviewed RFE's role in the affair,[14] the Council of Europe Special Committee submitted a closely reasoned report of the whole matter to the Consultative Assembly of the Council of Europe, and RFE investigated itself.[15]

Analysis of the broadcasts and interviews with escapees yielded a general exculpation of RFE as a prime causal factor in the revolution, or in any way promising the Hungarians what could not be delivered: armed American troops. Konrad Adenauer's investigating committee, alarmed that RFE's broadcasts were originating on West German soil, recognized the need to determine whether or not RFE was guilty as charged.

> "A verification has taken place," it wrote. "This verification revealed that the statements which appeared in the press that Radio Free Europe had promised armed support of the West to the Hungarians are not in conformity with the facts. Remarks have, however, been made which could give rise to a wrong interpretation. A debate and an exchange of views have therefore taken place which resulted in a turnover in the staff and I think that until further orders the matter may be considered closed." [16]

While seeming to settle the matter conclusively, the words "which could give rise to a wrong interpretation" pose more questions than they answer. RFE claims to this day that its organization was no more culpable in the Hungarian drama than the West at large; that, because Hungarians were angry at the United States for standing idly by at their moment of despair, they focused their ire on RFE, a privately run radio service. (It is estimated that the RFE audience dropped 25 per cent immediately after the uprising.) The blame, if indeed blame can be attached to anyone, is a collective one shared by the West in general.

It is still possible, however, to have reservations about RFE in the light of a number of key considerations. Holt notes in his book on RFE that Leonard Doob, an outstanding specialist in propaganda, domestic and international, has this to say about RFE:

"But such a station has one tremendous disadvantage which in my opinion is more important than all the advantages which I can think of: even though it is privately owned and even though directly or indirectly it emphasizes this fact in its broadcasts, its listeners are likely not to make a fine distinction. It has something to do with America, therefore it is America, which means the *American Government* [Italics ours]." [17]

What Doob is driving at is a fundamental point in mass persuasion and one that clarifies the role of RFE in the Hungarian uprising. *People tend to hear what they want to hear regardless of what is said.* The Hungarian people, therefore, straining under the yoke of communism, interpreted the RFE broadcasts (which did not openly suggest, or promise American aid in case of, revolt) to mean that they *should* rebel and that the Americans *would* help them. In this sense, then—if Doob's point is well taken—RFE was very much involved in the Hungarian affair. But it is also fair to assume that almost any communication from the free world (Voice of America or the BBC, for instance) might have had the same effect, RFE was simply the most popular, most highly regarded voice of the West, and therefore most likely to encourage unfounded assumptions in the satellite nations.

The Hungarian situation is not the only difficult one with

which RFE has to contend. Critics have sniped at it on other grounds. James Burnham, writing in the ultra-conservative *National Guardian*, sees the organization as a hotbed of spies. He writes:

> Continuing scandals—zealously kept from the notice of the U. S. taxpayers, who pay the bills—rock the multi-million dollar Radio Free Europe organization. . . . Within the past four years a dozen of RFE's Czech staff have defected to the East. RFE retained M. F. Machacek as its Czech representative in Paris for two years after the French police reported him as an enemy agent, until he too (in 1958) jumped the Curtain. The Bavarian government is so skeptical about RFE people that it refuses them entry to refugee camps.[18]

His charges, of course, are difficult either to confirm or refute. RFE is aware that it is probably infiltrated by Communist agents in spite of all attempts to screen employees with extreme care. In 1958 atropine, a deadly poison, was discovered in the salt shakers at RFE's Munich employees' cafeteria, but no one was injured and nothing significant seems to have ensued after the incident, except that the cafeteria was closed down for a time.[19] How the poison got into the salt remains a mystery.

Radio Free Europe keeps broadcasting, and looks forward, oddly enough, to the day when it will be liquidated. According to a spokesman, that will be when and if the five nations which receive its broadcasts achieve the right of self-determination and freedom. It is likely to be in business a long time.

Similar to RFE, but less well-known and more perplexing as a propaganda proposition, for reasons which will become clearer later in our discussion, is Radio Liberty, another privately sponsored international broadcasting organization.[20] In fact, as far as output is concerned, Radio Liberty boasts transmitters of greater over-all intensity than any other Western propaganda agency, public or private: 1,530,000 watts of electronic power delivered to the airwaves by seventeen puissant short-wave transmitters in Germany, on Formosa, and via relay stations in the Mediterranean.

Radio Liberty's target is the Soviet Union and garrisons of Russian soldiers wherever they are stationed. Its output is enormous. Broadcasting in seventeen languages of the USSR, it is on the air twenty-four hours a day ever day of the year, a total of about 1,666 transmissions a week.

Radio Liberty's total staff around the world numbers somewhere between 830 and 1,000 people, including twenty-five correspondents in various strategic areas and 200 former Soviet citizens who prepare and deliver the actual broadcasts. The organization has two main offices, one in New York City comprising the full floor of an office building on West Forty-second Street, the other in a reconstructed former airport building in Oberweisenfeld outside Munich, Germany.

What does Radio Liberty find to fill all this air time? According to spokesmen for the organization, it dedicates itself to telling the truth to the peoples of the USSR. This truth, of course—like most truths—is highly selective. Radio Liberty broadcasts ideas, facts, and program services which listeners would be unlikely to encounter on the rigidly controlled Soviet broadcasting system. News like Khrushchev's speech denouncing Stalin to the Twentieth Party Congress, a reading of Boris Pasternak's *Dr. Zhivago,* and essays by one-time Yugoslav Communist leader Milovan Djilas constitute the kind of thing that Radio Liberty is anxious to bring to Russians—as well as to expose them to pro-Western views and blasts at the present administration of the USSR. Radio Liberty also provides economic news, religious programming, and satire.

Incorporated under the laws of the Federal Republic of

Germany, Radio Liberty's émigré (or escapee) staff take the line that they are talking to fellow countrymen. They address Soviet citizens as "we" Russians or Turkmen or Uzbeks. Radio Liberty's staff also monitors more than 100 Soviet radio stations to keep up with currents of thought and interest in the USSR.

If it has done nothing else, Radio Liberty has at least annoyed Soviet officials. More than 299 jamming transmitters in the USSR attempt to muffle its voice, and have been at it since ten minutes after broadcasting started on March 1, 1953. Radio Liberty has attempted to handle this situation by increasing its power and by the use of other electronic gadgetry, but it has never had a vacation from the jammers, even at times when US-Soviet relations began to "thaw."

Radio Liberty has been roundly vilified in the Soviet press since December, 1954, and has even been the subject of Russian ire on the floor of the UN General Assembly. It was "honored" also by no less a personage than Foreign Minister Shepilov, who assailed it in a speech before the Supreme Soviet of the USSR. Soviet secret agents are said to have murdered two Radio Liberty writers, and many of the organization's personnel have been threatened by the Russians in one way or another. Something of an atmosphere of derring-do, proverbial cloak-and-dagger espionage, and Slavic intrigue surrounds the entire operation.

The organization claims that its efforts are highly effective, basing its conclusion mostly on mail it receives, from which it quotes copiously on behalf of its own propaganda. Since there are fourteen to fifteen million short-wave receivers in the USSR, it is possible that Radio Liberty has quite a large listening audience, despite jamming, government attacks, and reprisals against individuals who listen to foreign broadcasts. Five hundred and ninety-five interviews with individuals who had come from the Soviet Union during 1960 indicated that this was the case.

To speak of the "effectiveness" of Radio Liberty raises a host of problems similar to those posed by RFE. No scrutiny of this organization is adequate without considering these problems realistically. Radio Liberty is actually one of two projects of an organization called the American Committee for Liberation. Boasting a Board of Trustees including such distinguished citizens as Philip Willkie and the Hon. Charles Edison, the American Committee's first president was Eugene Lyons, now a senior editor of *The Reader's Digest*. The present head is Howland H. Sargeant, a former Assistant Secretary of State for Public Affairs during the Truman administration. He is in charge of policy for the organization.

What is unclear is precisely where the funds for the American Committee for Liberation come from. Unlike Radio Free Europe, Radio Liberty conducts no fund-raising campaigns. Yet the gigantic sums needed to run the organization are provided, according to the organization itself, from "foundations and public contributions"—and there the matter seems to rest as far as the general public is concerned. Whether any Western governments give covert aid to the American Committee, and who the interested parties behind it may be, are not, in fact, on the public record and require no conjecture here.

In addition to Radio Liberty, the American Committee for Liberation sponsors the Institute for the Study of the USSR. Let this organization speak for itself in terms of its function and nature:

> The Institute for the Study of the USSR is a body of émigré scholars from the Soviet Union, whose aim is to furnish reliable information regarding conditions and trends in the Soviet Union. *Founded in 1950, its activities are centered in Munich,*

*Germany. The official membership consists of about fifty émi-
gré scholars drawn from various nationality groups making up
the Soviet Union. Its studies cover the general field of the behavioral sciences, including various aspects of economics, law,
government and Party, history, education, religion, literature
and social organization and dynamics.*

ACTIVITIES

The results of Institute research are disseminated through
publications, replies to requests for information, and conferences. The publications include a wide range of periodicals,
monographs, conference reports, and miscellaneous materials.
Publications are in various world languages. . . .

The periodicals are supplemented by monographic studies
of varied scope, appearing in various languages. . . .

The Institute provides an information service under which
answers are provided to outside inquiries. Special arrangements may be made for more extensive research projects.

A final method for providing reliable factual information
regarding the Soviet Union is that of conferences. A large annual conference is held in Munich, usually in July. . . .

RESOURCES

The research studies which provide the materials for publication are based on unexcelled resources. . . .

The resident research staff has at its disposal the largest
library in Europe specializing in Soviet materials alone. The
library consists of over 37,000 books and 11,000 volumes of
newspapers and periodicals, in Russian and other languages. It
is kept current by regular acquisition of practically everything
available in the field of Soviet behavioral sciences. Non-Soviet
materials are acquired in smaller degree, and are supplemented
locally by the resources of the various Munich library collec-
tions.

Finally, the Institute has at its disposal an experienced staff
of émigré and non-émigré technical research and publication
specialists such as editors, proofreaders, multi-language typists,
librarians and so on.[21]

The Institute has also prepared a series of fifteen-minute radio programs, broadcast in the United States over the Mutual radio network and entitled "The Anatomy of Soviet Communism." These deal with various aspects of life in the USSR —religion, foreign policy, and the arts—scripts of which are published in booklets available to the public.[22]

Needless to say, most, if not all, of the inquiries undertaken by the Institute for the Study of the USSR are pretty rough on communism and the present Russian leaders. A bleak picture is painted in their publications of all aspects of Soviet life. Nor do they give much credence to material and educational advances which—like it or not—are hard facts that have marked the years since the Russian Revolution, before which many Russians were living in ways more appropriate to the Middle Ages than to the twentieth century. Little of this positive aspect of Soviet life or culture finds its way into the Institute's publications. While the Institute provides a good deal of excellent documentation revealing the ubiquity of cracks in the Kremlin wall, one wonders whether there are any similar institutes inside the USSR for the study of the United States, and what kinds of documentation they might come up with in regard to American cultural, political, and social weaknesses!

Like Radio Free Europe, the American Committee for Liberation faces a fundamental problem in terms of its specific objectives. Having solved most of its operational difficulties, it is still pretty vague on exactly what it hopes to accomplish in propaganda terms. Since it is not an official arm of government, it is free to operate irrespective of American foreign policy, which a government propaganda agency such as the USIA cannot afford to do. On the other hand, the Committee cannot afford to veer too far from the best interests and policies of the United States Government. First, it is committed to loyalty to the free world; second, listeners in the Soviet Union will probably interpret Radio Liberty's programs in the same way that listeners in satellite nations regard RFE—, namely, as *official* American broadcasts. They are not likely to understand that Radio Liberty is directed by private citizens whose aims may or may not coordinate with government policy.

Symbolic of this problem is the change made in 1959 in the very name of the broadcasting service. From 1953 to that year, it had been called "Radio Liberation," a term carrying a military flavor both in English and in Russian, and connoting a specific objective for the programs: the eventual overthrow of Soviet dictatorship. The change to "Radio Liberty"—a softer implication—may well indicate a blunting of the aims of the American Committee for Liberation, based upon a realistic recognition that it is unlikely that the Russian people will disturb a ruling regime which has given them a slowly but surely achieved increased prosperity and the psychological shot in the arm of scientific excellence in space technology. The idea for the change in the name of the organization came, incidentally, from Russian refugee employees who recognized the inappropriateness of the former appellation.

It does not seem to be in the cards that a revolution of any sort will occur in the reasonably foreseeable future in the USSR, and Radio Liberty has to face this fact—just as Radio Free Europe has to square up to the realization that its apparently clear over-all objective, freedom for Iron Curtain countries, would be the end product it would least welcome if this were attempted prematurely or in unpropitious circumstances. This is the lesson RFE has unquestionably learned from the Hungarian Revolution which, had it embroiled the Western powers, might well have triggered World War III.

Does this mean that RFE and Radio Liberty have no

function in the international arena in the coming years? Decidedly not. Propaganda, especially constructive propaganda, may have a vital role even if it does not foment revolutions. It can influence public opinion and thereby smooth the path for our diplomats in obtaining significant concessions. It can help captive nations and Soviet citizens to extract freedoms from the ruling oligarchs which would otherwise be denied to them; occasionally it can even embarrass Communist governments into printing the truth about themselves and world affairs in their state-controlled presses. Lastly, and most important, it can help the rank-and-file citizens to keep alive the image of and hope for freedom and justice.

James Webb Young in the *Saturday Review*[23] suggests that we in the free world establish a College of Propaganda to train people in the arts of persuasion—a first-rate idea. Radio Free Europe and Radio Liberty are almost certain to remain in business for many years to come, and the people who operate them are going to need plenty of excellent and intensive preparation. To go through the next decade without the services of skilled and knowledgeable idea invaders bringing the Voice of Freedom to the millions living under Communist tyranny would be a chilling prospect. Our own survival may well depend on how effectively we can communicate with the enslaved satellites and the Russian people themselves.

UNCLE SAM'S SOFT SELL

We can work our hearts out for years building up goodwill for the United States in a given country when suddenly one little policy action is taken which does more to destroy our position than the USIA can rebuild in a very long time. I want to make it absolutely clear that I am not writing down the importance of the U. S. Information Agency. I am writing up the importance of having the public relations aspects of policy taken into consideration when policy is made.

—GEORGE V. ALLEN in a talk to USIA employees, 1957 [1]

We are now in a period when the mission and style of diplomacy are changing. These changes reflect technical developments in transport and communications, the growing role of public opinion in world affairs, and the practices of the Soviet propaganda apparatus. Our diplomacy increasingly must give greater emphasis to the factor of public opinion in the handling of major conferences and negotiations.

—Recommendation to President Eisenhower by Mansfield D. Sprague, Chairman of the President's Committee on Information Activities Abroad [2]

WHERE international affairs are concerned, nothing is more understandable than a wistful affection for the "good old days." Sir Harold Nicolson, whose career in diplomacy and letters stretches from the Edwardian era to the present, observes, "Traditional diplomacy, at its best, was courteous and dignified; it was continuous and gradual; it attached importance to knowledge and experience; it took account of the realities of existing power; and it defined good faith, lucidity and precision as the qualities essential to any sound negotiation." One can almost hear Sir Harold sigh as he goes on to observe, "In the days of the old diplomacy it would have been an act of unthinkable vulgarity to appeal to the common people upon any issue of international policy." [3]

How things have changed since Sir Harold's day! As we have seen, new problems arise from technological advances in communications and transportation, the development of modern propaganda, the threat of total warfare, and the growing importance of "public opinion" about which, in one degree or another, all diplomatic chess players in the international arena must be concerned. The fact that international relations have changed more radically in the past forty years than in all the centuries before is a familiar theme whose significance can hardly be over-emphasized.

The complexity and scope of the new frontiers of communication challenge the imagination. The concept of idea invasion is by no means new, but its extraordinary dimensions today are novel indeed, giving the art of propaganda a distinctive and original quality. For the first time in the history of the world, no government can afford not to be in the business of mass persuasion. The United States is no exception.

Our entry into this field was belated and reluctant.[4] Our participation is still somewhat unwilling, as evidenced by our insistence on euphemizing our propaganda arm into an "information" agency. But Uncle Sam had to wake up eventually to the demands of the twentieth century, and the United States Information Agency is the result.

Our first flirtation with propaganda techniques occurred during World War I, when we established the Committee on Public Information (or the Creel Committee) under George Creel.[5] It was the job of this agency, created by President Woodrow Wilson, to whip up morale on the home front and to wage psychological warfare against the enemy. Since we thought of propaganda as strictly a wartime measure, and since we were distressingly eager to stick our heads in the sand after the conflict, the Committee went out of business in 1919. Americans simply didn't give a hoot about selling America abroad. There seemed to be no need for that kind of effort.

The first government agencies to be concerned with propaganda or information (the terms will be used interchangeably below) in peacetime were established by President Roosevelt's Department of State in 1938. The Interdepartmental Committee for Scientific and Cultural Cooperation was an advisory agency for the Division of Cultural Cooperation, and both represented the functional arm of President Roosevelt's Pan-American unity program, centering their activities in South and Central America. The Office of the Coordinator for Inter-American Affairs was set up as a separate agency in 1941. The two former bodies were headed by Nelson Rockefeller and accented a "good-neighbor" policy in radio broadcasts, newspaper articles, and the like toward all of Latin America.

Then came World War II and the effective beginnings of what was later to become the United States Information Agency. With war clouds gathering, Roosevelt authorized Colonel "Wild Bill" Donovan (later of OSS fame) to set up a Foreign Information Service under presidential speech writer and playwright, Robert E. Sherwood. The Japanese bombed Pearl Harbor in December of that year, and by the end of February Sherwood was broadcasting on short-wave radio as the "Voice of America." Dizard quotes the following statement by Sherwood as our first official attempt at international propaganda in World War II. "The Voice speaks," said Sherwood. "Today America has been at war for seventy-nine days. Daily at this time we shall speak to you about America and the war. The news may be good or bad. We shall tell you the truth." [6] And that is what the "Voice" has been doing more or less ever since.

Also arriving in Washington in 1941 was poet Archibald MacLeish, head of the Office of Facts and Figures, whose job it was to inform the American people on the progress of the war effort. According to many observers, however, the FIS and OFF got pretty well fouled up in the snares of bureaucracy, and in June, 1942, both were consolidated into the Office of War Information under the direction of veteran newsman Elmer Davis with the aim of administering a war information program at home and overseas. [7]

Despite the lack of coordination between the State Department and the agency—and the strange fact that OWI's headquarters were based in New York, not in Washington, thus creating a communication snafu of some proportions—Davis created a complex wartime propaganda agency literally out of nothing. It is generally conceded that the OWI did its best job overseas, where its posts operated as the United States Information Service, but it had numerous functions at home as well as abroad.

In characteristically American fashion, at war's end we were all too eager to get out of the propaganda business, unaware of the impending cold war that was just around the corner. OWI had been attacked during World War II by Congressmen and columnists as a political forum for left-wingers and other subversives, and in August, 1945, before the atomic dust had settled at Hiroshima, the order came through to disband the 13,000 man organization by New Year's Day.

At the urging, however, of such foresighted individuals as the then Assistant Secretary of State William H. Benton, Secretary of State George C. Marshall, and President Truman, the axe was stayed—or at least the blow was softened—and a skeleton organization in the form of various interim agencies was maintained until 1947. The government continued the Voice of America broadcasts on a considerably curtailed basis, published one Russian-language magazine, and conducted motion picture and newspaper propaganda on a relatively minor scale.

In the years between it became clear that, however much we might want to keep away from international propaganda and whatever risks such propaganda involved, the greatest danger by far lay in non-participation in what was to become a cold war of words. Faced with the articulate Soviet persuasion that blanketed neutral and friendly nations, we saw how

the battle lines of the cold war were being drawn and we recognized that, like it or not, we could not afford to stay out of
the verbal struggle.

The passage of the Smith-Mundt Act of 1948 gave the
government $30 million to build up our propaganda program
to be administered by career diplomat George V. Allen. By
1951, as part of President Truman's Campaign of Truth, the
appropriation for it was nearly tripled. Under various names
the agency operated as part of the State Department; by 1952
it was called the International Information Administration.

About this time the late Senator Joseph McCarthy of Wis-
consin began his flagrant attack on the agency, promising the
public that he would unearth radicals, homosexuals, traitors,
and all sorts of other vermin in the State Department. It was
during this period that his boy-wonder assistant, lawyer Roy
Cohn, and the then G. I. David Schine swept through the
overseas libraries of the USIS, finding such subversive books
as *The Maltese Falcon* on their shelves.

McCarthy's high jinks actually served the USIA well in the
end, because after the function of the agency was publicized
and it succeeded in showing conclusively that it was not rid-
dled with Reds or incompetents, the Senate Foreign Relations
Committee recommended the formation of a separate body to
carry on our information program. Thus was the United States
Information Agency born on August 1, 1953.[8] Operating in-
dependently of the Department of State, but receiving policy
guidance from it, the new organization recognized the expedi-
ency of moving its headquarters from New York to Washington.[9]

The USIA is today part of the executive branch of our
government, one of a group of units such as the White House
Office and the Council of Economic Advisors, whose directors
report directly to the President. Appropriations for USIA are

voted yearly by Congress and have ranged from roughly $85 million in 1954 to nearly $150 million in 1963. Over 12,000 persons work for USIA at home and abroad; it is an agency of enormous complexity, neither exempt from the weaknesses nor slow to benefit from the strengths of Big Government.[10]

On the debit side of the ledger, immensity and complexity lead to bureaucracy and complacency, the inculcation of a kind of mentality which seeks out the safety of tradition and invokes the motto, "Don't rock the boat." On the credit side, USIA attracts a number of zealous people who are characterized both by a missionary spirit and knowledge of how to carry out their important and intricate tasks. The present director of the USIA, Edward R. Murrow, is quoted as saying that he was pleasantly surprised by the quality and competence of the staff of the agency when he took office. "There's a lot of ability, experience and depth of dedication in this place" [11] was his comment.

The objectives of the USIA have, of course, been stated many times, and in formulating them great pains have invariably been taken to cloak them in phrases which (1) cannot be interpreted exclusively as self-interest on the part of the USA, and (2) which will maintain the "educational" aura around the agency's activities. Dizard summarizes them neatly:

> 1. To provide an image of the United States as a leader in the free world whose fundamental interests are similar to those of other free world countries.
> 2. To document American life as a reflection of a vigorous democratic society whose goals are similar to those of other free world nations.
> 3. In countries where the United States has economic and military aid programs, to publicize the extent and purpose of these programs.
> 4. To point up, where necessary, the danger of Communism as a new form of imperialism that threatens the freedom of

independent nations through internal subversion and external aggression.[12]

The specific ways in which the USIA implements these objectives are so variegated, widespread, and complicated that they could not be described short of book length.[13] Suffice it to note here that there are five major arms of the organization: staff offices, program services, geographic offices (all of them located in the United States), and the overseas operations which include United States Information Service posts, radio relay centers, and press service centers. About one-quarter of the USIA's staff is based in the United States. The rest are stationed abroad, where about five-sixths are local employees.

The main functions of the organization are carried out by the various branches, to each of which is delegated a certain kind of responsibility according to either specific objectives or the medium utilized to achieve them. The Office of Private Cooperation, for instance, concentrates on working with private citizens, private business groups, service organizations, philanthropic institutions, secondary schools, cities, and universities in supporting the programs of the USIA posts overseas. To this end, it offers courses for business executives who travel abroad, encourages a "Books From America" project which distributes American reading matter in foreign lands, provides government liaison for our hospital training ship "Hope," and engages in other activities of this nature.

The Press and Publication Service, on the other hand, is a world-wide press service which operates printing plants in Manila and Beirut, runs a world-wide radio teletypewriter communications system, and furnishes photo reproduction services. Supplementing rather than competing with private American news sources such as the Associated Press and United Press International, its output comprises a galaxy of pamphlets, magazines, and news releases, including approximately 10,000 words of daily news from the United States. Magazines in Russian, Polish, English, Spanish, and Arabic are prepared in Washington in addition to more than seventy-five other magazines and newspapers edited overseas.

Motion picture propaganda is handled by the Motion Picture Service, which produces documentaries, newsreels, and shorts on various aspects of American life to be shown by foreign theaters and television stations under the auspices of foreign service agencies and at USIA Information Centers. All in all, this unit mans 210 film libraries in 98 countries, each library containing from 500 to 1,000 films both in English and in the language of the country in which it is housed. To facilitate the showing of these films, the USIA has nearly 8,000 projectors in use overseas, as well as 260 mobile units for nations where electricity or meeting halls are not readily available. The Motion Picture Service estimates that some 600 million people see USIA films each month. It also sends abroad each month more than 475 television programs on film; some of these are produced by the USIA and others are acquired from commercial broadcasters.

The virtual backbone of the USIA is its Information Center Service. There are over 200 employees on the domestic staff of this division; another 200 are based overseas and the remaining foreign staff numbers over 1,000. The ICS runs 176 libraries in eighty countries—mostly friendly or neutral nations—which circulate eight million books annually. In addition, the overseas centers sponsor courses in English, distribute books in many languages (apart from those circulated by the libraries), hold exhibits and concerts, and act, in general, as a cultural arm of the agency. In this connection they set themselves the task of slaking the insatiable curiosity of foreign nationals about the USA and provide help for scholars, researchers, and the like.

These information posts unquestionably represent America effectively in the minds of people overseas. Dizard notes[14] that one hazard of service in the USIA is that when resentment against the United States reaches riot proportions, it is almost invariably a USIA post which is first attacked by insurgents. Because of the vastly different challenges facing the various missions around the globe, each post varies its *modus operandi* according to the local political climate and on-the-spot pressures. In general, though, each post is divided into two working units, one concerned mostly with information—that is, dissemination of materials for media of communications— the other with cultural matters and attempts to keep up to date on local currents of thought so that the aims and goals of the USA may be interpreted to the foreign intellectual élite.

Parenthetically, a distinction must be pointed out between the USIA and the USIS. The United States Information Agency is operative in the United States and is the planning bureau for over-all strategy. The United States Information Service is the designation given to the foreign posts of the agency which are maintained *throughout the world*.

The most familiar arm of the USIA, at home at least, is its radio service, the Voice of America, which has kept the name given it by Sherwood back in the early days of World War II. It comprises today a gigantic international radio network run by our government that broadcasts in a total of sixty-four languages (fifty-two of which are used on a regular basis) by means of eighty-seven powerful transmitters. Fifty-five of these are located overseas, including one mounted on the United States Coast Guard cutter "Courier" presently anchored at Rhodes. VOA programs are also "spotted" into local broadcast facilities and reach an estimated forty-five million people per day in addition to the twenty million or so listeners to their short-wave service.

Budgeted at more than $20 million, the VOA alone employs about 1,000 persons here in the USA (where most of the programs originate) and about 700 overseas, most of whom are involved in the technical end of the operation. The VOA is on the air, over various frequencies, for about 715 hours a week.[15] Many of its programs are repeated two or more times a day and most are prepared in its elaborate studios located on the second floor of the Health, Education and Welfare Building in Washington, D. C.

As for its goals, the VOA, of course, is charged with implementing the objectives of the USIA, which, in turn, receives its major policy directives—despite the implications of the previous quotation cited by Dizard—from the Department of State. The following directive concerns the decorum and responsibilities of VOA broadcasters:

> The long-range interests of the United States are served by communicating directly with the peoples of the world by radio. To be effective, the Voice of America must win the attention and respect of listeners. These principles will govern VOA broadcasts:
>
> 1. VOA will establish itself as a consistently reliable and authoritative source of news. VOA news will be accurate, objective, and comprehensive.
>
> 2. VOA will represent America, not any single segment of American society. It will therefore present a balanced and comprehensive projection of significant American thought and institutions.[15a]
>
> 3. As an official radio service, VOA will present the policies of the United States clearly and effectively. VOA will also present responsible discussion and opinion on these policies.[16]

The Voice attempts to accomplish these ends in numerous ways. On a typical day, it beams programs in a host of languages to just about every nation on the globe. A typical program schedule selected at random is the VOA's broadcasts to the Middle East during February, March, and April, 1962. It includes the following material taken directly from a VOA program brochure, with only frequency directions omitted.

THE CHALLENGE AND THE CONFRONTATION:

A series of programs which will examine in positive form those areas in the world in which free choice has rejected communism completely or has set back the doctrine of the inevitability of the Communist system.

THE AMERICAN SMALL BUSINESSMAN:

These programs will picture, in documentary form, businessmen, shopkeepers and service people who have been able, through the exercise of free choice, to develop their own individual patterns of life.

THE U.N. SPECIALIZED AGENCIES:

Broadcasts consist of programs, in semi-documentary form, on the work of the specialized agencies of the United Nations.

AGRICULTURE SERIES:

Will present new developments in American agriculture that should be of interest to listeners overseas.

MUSICAL LIFE IN THE UNITED STATES:

A series of programs presenting prominent symphony orchestras of the United States, concert and opera artists, American composers, music festivals, music from conservatories, community musical activities, American operas and other significant musical activities.

NEWS IN SPECIAL ENGLISH:

This is a specially designed newscast using a limited vocabulary of approximately 1200 words prepared for our listeners who are developing English as a second language. World news is broadcast Monday through Saturday at 2100 GMT at a reduced speed to enable our audience to follow the announcer with a minimum of difficulty.

HAVE YOU A QUESTION?:

This program welcomes questions from Voice of America listeners on any phase of life in the United States. Send your question to: Question Editor, Voice of America, Washington, D.C., U.S.A. If your question is used on the program, you will receive a copy of the American Heritage *Book of Great Historic Places,* which contains hundreds of color pictures illustrating highlights of American history.

COMMON CAUSE:

Report on how the people of the United States join with the peoples of other lands in the fight against poverty, illiteracy and disease.[17]

One finds also in this schedule such rich and variegated radio fare as "Sports Arena," "Report to Youth," "The Arts in the United States," "The Feminine Touch," jazz, folk music, science programs, and the songs of Bing Crosby. It is reassuring to note the general excellence of these offerings.

The VOA's three mainstays are news, commentary, and music. The anchor man on its English-language news broadcasts is Raymond G. Swing, whose precise diction and unemotional evaluations of world crises are familiar to many Americans as the result of his services on the home front during World War II. The VOA's main purveyor of music is a disc jockey named Willis Conover whose program, "Music USA" is the most popular item on the VOA's bill of fare. Although relatively unfamiliar in America, Conover is probably one of the best known and best liked broadcasters in the world. The music chosen to represent the USA is popular music and jazz—mercifully excluding, for the most part, rock 'n' roll and other atonal and cacophonous noises which are likely to be misinterpreted by foreign listeners.[18] Like Radio Liberty and Radio Free Europe, the VOA is naturally jammed behind the Iron Curtain. Communists rationalize this practice as an attempt to defend themselves against psychological aggression and interference with their internal affairs. Although jamming was condemned by the General Assembly of the United Nations in 1950 and the object of a free world complaint at the Foreign Ministers' Conference in Geneva in 1955, the jamming of VOA broadcasts to Russia and satellite countries continues unabated. When asked why this was being done, Khrushchev replied disingenuously:

> If the Voice of America does become the voice of America —because we respect the American people—it will not be jammed in our country; but when it is not the voice of America but a sort of wailing over the radio supposedly the voice of America, in that case we want to avoid our people getting the wrong view of the American people.[19]

The Soviets do not jam all VOA broadcasts, however, since they have shrewdly decided to let programs go through from which they expect to reap a propaganda advantage. Anything from any source that directly or indirectly casts discredit upon the West and builds up Russian prestige is now turned to account. This practice dates from Khrushchev's visit to the United States in 1959, when the VOA was heard in the Soviet Union with perfect clarity. Incidentally, VOA programs in local languages are interfered with much more frequently than those in English. Since 1958 the Chinese Communists have copied the Russian pattern of selective jamming.

It is estimated that if the United States were to purchase transmitters comparable to those used by the communists for jamming alone, the initial investment would be about $250 million, and it would cost another $185 million a year to operate them. At present the USA spends only about $150 million a year for all its international propaganda activities, of which radio is just one part. The seriousness, therefore, with which the USSR views Western broadcasts is clearly evident. At any rate, despite the intensity of Soviet interference and the fact that much radio listening behind the Iron Curtain is done on wired receivers incapable of picking up broadcast frequencies, the VOA estimates that satisfactory reception ranges from 40 per cent to 95 per cent, so that a considerable proportion of the VOA's programs are available and listened to in Iron Curtain nations.

The USIA has its fingers in the pie of two other international broadcasting services as well. RIAS (or Radio in American Sector) is one of them. Also a heritage of World War II, RIAS began broadcasting in Berlin in 1946 owing to the fact that the Soviets had pretty well taken over Radio Berlin. RIAS is today the German arm of the USIS and one of its most effective means of reaching the East German audience. The staff of RIAS is largely German, and the station broadcasts news, commentary, educational offerings, and general programming (including comedies which satirize Soviet life) twenty-four hours a day. Bitterly attacked by East German officials and newspapers and frequently jammed, there is much evidence that RIAS is one of the most popular stations operating in Germany today. In one month alone in 1946 it received 75,000 letters from listeners in the Eastern zone. It has been credited with a substantial role in encouraging defection of East Germans to the West. Only a minor part of its programming is provided by the VOA; most originates from Berlin and is geared closely to German tastes and interests.[20]

While RIAS is the only station that the USIA operates on foreign soil, the VOA's facilities are also made available for the Armed Forces Radio and Television Service. It is impossible to conjecture as to the extent to which this network serves the United States as a propaganda agency, but it probably has some effect in spreading abroad an understanding of the lighter aspects of American life, as portrayed by "Bob and Ray," Rosemary Clooney, and others. Designed for service personnel abroad, its range of programming attracts a considerable number of non-service, English-speaking listeners. Most of the broadcasting on AFRTS comes from commercial sources in the United States, although some is prepared by its own staff consisting both of armed forces personnel and civilians.

An outstanding example of how the facilities of the USIA can be used for mass persuasion is found in the handling of the Cuban crisis during the fall of 1962.[21] The agency's answer to the challenge of convincing Latin America and the rest of the world that the USA had no choice but to call Castro and the Russians to account for the missile build-up on Cuba was efficient, instantaneous, and extensive in scope.

First of all, President Kennedy's address to the American people was transmitted by short wave and on standard radio frequencies—with the assist of a number of American private stations—to the entire world, with particular emphasis on Spanish-language broadcasts to Cuba and the nations of South and Central America. The latter countries received numerous video tapes and films of the President's appearance, each dubbed in its own language for theatrical and non-theatrical showing.

The agency's many posts overseas were busy all the while translating the talk for distribution to local newspapers and government officials, including in their "hand-out" prints, negatives, and plates of the dramatic aerial photographs of the Russian missile sites. The USIA had also prepared a number of short TV programs on Cuba and the Castro regime which were rushed to video outlets in Latin America and elsewhere.

In addition, the USIA acquired a commercial TV program, "Anatomy of Betrayal," which was translated into

Spanish and Portuguese, while fifty-two transmitters located in the vicinity of the Soviet Union broadcast the full story of the Cuban situation to people in Iron Curtain countries.

All these instrumentalities—and more—were marshalled brilliantly by the USIA in meeting the most serious emergency yet to have arisen in the cold war. Coupled with distribution of news releases, photographs, specially prepared background pamphlets, and other materials, the USIA's broadcasting activities constituted perhaps the most massive and comprehensive propaganda operations in the history of the agency. Without this far-flung persuasion campaign, America's position in this delicate balance of international tensions could not have been carried around the world and the magnitude of our success in this instance would have been correspondingly decreased.

Needless to say, the USIA is not without its critics. Little objection is made to its motives or objectives, but some misgivings are occasionally voiced as to the means and methods it has adopted in pursuit of its ends. *Newsweek* magazine quotes Arthur Larson,[22] a past director of the USIA, as being critical of the shortage of USIA employees overseas who are conversant with the native tongues of the nations where they are assigned. Harold Lasswell, an authority on psychological warfare, views the organization as "a body of hurried men attempting to put forth good faith on emergency solutions," and C. D. Jackson, a man instrumental in the creation of the USIA, bemoans the fact that a propaganda agency speaking for our government can be only as effective as our government's policies. Since USIA is usually impotent in the formation of these policies, its operations, says Jackson, leave much to be desired.

Like Jackson, James Reston of the *New York Times*[23] has noted that the USIA is powerless to initiate United States pol-

icy and when that policy constitutes bad propaganda, the
USIA has no alternative but to broadcast it far and wide. Our
resumption of nuclear testing (in response to Soviet provoca-
tion when the USSR broke faith and set off giant bombs) is a
case in point: spreading the news did little to enhance our national image as a peaceful nation, but the USIA had no alternative but to tell the world about our decision.

One of the most consistent critics of the USIA is columnist
David Lawrence. He frequently takes issue with the organization's "soft" line and objective presentation of material. It is
his opinion that a propaganda agency should propagandize
purely and simply. About the USIA's directives, he writes:

> [They] are based on a pussyfoot policy of forbearance.
> They provide that care should be taken not to seem to be deal-
> ing with internal affairs in Russia. So broadcasts are made
> in vague and abstract jargon, designed mostly to reach so-
> called "intellectuals." Highbrow lectures are offered to such
> an audience, when simple truths need to be stressed to pub-
> licize the current behavior of Khrushchev.[24]

While some of Lawrence's points are well taken, he is
more facile as a purveyor of destructive criticisms than as a
source of constructive suggestions. Demeaning our utterances
in the propaganda war to the level of the USSR's vicious in-
vectives hardly seems to be the answer to the problems he
poses. If the Russian idea invaders have an Achilles heel at all,
it is by virtue of the strain that Kremlin propaganda puts on
credulity and the fact that the number of people you can fool
all the time is mercifully limited.

Another blast at the USIA's present "soft" propaganda
policy appeared in the fall of 1962 in *Printers' Ink* magazine,[25]
a journal largely given over to reporting news of the advertising industry. Mincing no words, this unsigned piece hits
USIA policy on a number of specific points. "The USIA ranks

low on all the key elements in persuasion," says the magazine, as it goes on to list inadequate funds, incompetent employees, and a lack of clear definition of goals as its major problems.

What *Printers' Ink* seems to want is to turn Uncle Sam's propaganda activities over to the commercial advertisers, calling on what the magazine describes as "the skilled persuader" to "sell" America abroad. At least, the opinions of these "skilled persuaders" constitute much of the meat of the article. In their concrete suggestions for carrying on ideological warfare, they list a number of steps which reflect procedures derived from Madison Avenue and the world of the "hard sell," and advocate bringing into the government agency "researchers, communication leaders in all media, advertising and market specialists, educators, religious thinkers, economists, psychologists, sociologists, historians, etc."

The prospect of these "skilled specialists" at work in idea invasion of the sort we have been discussing, dealing with sensitive areas of world opinion and momentous issues far removed from the world of commercial exploitation, would be amusing if it were not so chilling. While some of *Printers' Ink*'s ideas are worthwhile—particularly about training propagandists and providing wider resources for American international persuasion—this well-written article is one further manifestation of the professional huckster's brashness in offering to help solve any and all problems of the body politic. What the advertising community seems incapable of understanding in regard to the USIA is that democracy and the American way of life cannot be sold like corn flakes and cigarettes, that foreigners are different from Americans, and that advertising is poles apart from ideological persuasion. Let us hope we do not have to learn this lesson in the crucible of bitter experience!

Charges of a somewhat different kind have been hurled at

the USIA by Donald Brandon, a former government employee overseas. He writes as follows in the *Commonweal:*

> The tenor of the Agency's message up to now has been self-righteous and aggressive, reflecting America's consternation at discovering that the United States is as disliked and feared as the Soviet Union in many countries. But this response has been self-defeating, and has only served to reaffirm the widely-held view that the United States is an immature, materialistic nation. . . .
>
> Furthermore, if USIA is to accomplish its objectives, its personnel as well as its program must be improved. Personal contacts with influential leaders of public opinion in other countries can be as valuable as the cultural program in gaining support for America and its policies, and the relatively few direct successes scored by the Agency have been the work of outstanding individuals rather than the result of the mass informational program. A survey of USIA's semi-annual reports to the Congress shows that the Agency itself highlights the achievements of a few officers who gained the confidence and respect of foreign leaders and thereby influenced either opinion or policy-making officials in a manner favorable to the United States.
>
> Unfortunately, the majority of rank and file USIA officers stationed abroad scoff at the cultural program and lack the sense of purpose and the skills required to develop meaningful contacts. Apart from the well-known language deficiencies of Agency personnel, far too many of them are in the foreign service primarily because of the opportunities for travel, security and status.[26]

He goes on to say that unless we can do more than take an "anti-Communist" stance—that is, articulate a more positive foreign policy than merely a stand against Russian aggression—there seems to be little of a constructive nature that the USIA's operations can accomplish.

Brandon's position was roundly attacked in a subsequent issue of the magazine, and there is considerable evidence that his allegations require qualification in the interests of fact.[27]

An important point is the formidable difficulty in staffing adequately so large a government organization, considering especially the range of current government salaries. As for the USIA's message being "self-righteous and aggressive," it is exactly the shortage of aggressiveness for which the USIA has many times been scored by critics of Mr. Lawrence's persuasion. These two accusations would seem to cancel each other out.

President Kennedy is evidently well aware of the USIA's shortcomings for he has created a five-man committee (on which Murrow sits) to try to increase the effectiveness of the agency.[28] President Eisenhower established a similar Operations Coordinating Board late in his administration, but the Democrats abolished it in the early days of the Kennedy Administration. Significantly, this board's Committee on Information Activities submitted a report[29] via its chairman, Mansfield D. Sprague, to the President (just as the Eisenhower Administration was on its way out), which was pretty hard on USIA methods. Briefly stated, the report suggested the expansion of our information activities, an improved training program, increased educational development overseas, new exchange programs, greater consideration of the effects of United States technical assistance abroad, and more attention to the selection of our Foreign Service personnel. Voicing a whole series of criticisms which were far from a vote of confidence in the *status quo,* the report said, in effect, that the USIA should actually do effectively and purposefully what it professes to do.

As armchair experts, the present authors can hardly evaluate fairly the USIA and its program. We have talked to its representatives, examined its scripts, listened to its broadcasts, and, in our travels, observed some of its activities overseas. We have also studied closely both its history and present role in the international scene. Yet the all-around efficacy of the USIA remains problematical even after such scrutiny, so complex and many-sided are the issues with which it must grapple in all corners of the globe.

Conclusions had therefore best be left to history. As we said at the outset of this chapter, the United States does not want—has never wanted—to be in the propaganda business. Our open society should be its own best propagandist. We are nevertheless engaged in a mortal struggle with an enemy who seeks to bury our ideals, is skilled in the most unscrupulous type of persuasion, and works tirelessly at subverting and controlling world public opinion.

This state of affairs is the central fact of the twentieth century. People everywhere are worried that a nuclear war may be triggered at any moment, either by accident or design. The USA and the Soviet Union are desperately afraid of each other's bombs. At present they have little left to do but talk, and talk they do—but unfortunately mostly to their allies and the "neutrals" and not to each other.

Meanwhile, both countries boast of their peaceful intentions. To a discerning listener, the raucousness of the Soviet is that of a carnival barker and its veracity reminiscent of a con man's. Our voice is softer, our message more objective and truthful. We must hope that our audience will in the end accept the quiet appeal to reason. That is what the USIA is betting on, and there is a good chance that it will work.

Our official agencies of propaganda must necessarily reflect our history, our traditions, and our faith in man and democracy. For us, no other course is conceivable; these are our broad outlines for checking and reversing the inroads of Soviet propaganda.

AMERICA, THE NOT-SO-BEAUTIFUL

I think that if we can get across to all of these peoples and to all of these countries what the United States is really about, what we stand for in this country, I think that we are going to win.

—ATTORNEY GENERAL ROBERT F. KENNEDY[1]

The categorical and radical utterances of which Americans are capable tend to make one forget that nowhere else in the world are contradictory ideals being reconciled by such wise and lasting compromises. The radicalism of the American is a radicalism of the tongue. It takes a long time for this to be understood by the observer of the American scene, and Americans themselves can give him but a little assistance, since they have grown up with their contradictions and consider them the most natural things in the world.

—PETER VON ZAHN[2]

Americans are hypocrites.

—A Danish student[3]

CHAPTER **10**

THERE is probably no national group which is collectively less conscious of its own nationality than the United States of America. Europeans are reminded of "who they are" in terms of nationality by the many borders on their continent and the ease with which armies can cross them. So-called backward nations are reminded of what it means to be a Ghana, a Vietnam, or a Burma by the ever-present drive—sometimes military—to establish their identity in the community of nations. Much the same psychology is at work in South American lands which deliberately cultivate qualities of national uniqueness. Iceland, Greenland, Portugal, and the like are similarly motivated, and Canada and Mexico have both been impelled to formulate a clear self-image as a means of resisting the encroaching economic and cultural forces of the United States.

Americans, however, have had trouble forming a clear national image of themselves at least since World War I, after which the previously idealized vision of America as the "melting pot where all the races of Europe are melting and reforming. . . ." [4] was blurred by immigration laws, and the ideal was relegated to anthologies of poems for tots to read in public elementary schools. Something of a concrete American identity was achieved for a short time during World War II, but this was largely a reactive phenomenon: outrage at Pearl Harbor, the caprices and inhumanities of Hitler, an offended sense of fair play,[5] and sympathy for the "plucky" British and the citizens of the captive lands. Americans identified themselves with the traditions of chivalry in the Western world at large rather than with a credo distinctly American. We were not, as were our fathers in World War I, out to "make the world safe for democracy" (largely an American slogan), but rather to create a world in which the "Four Freedoms" could become realities. And the Four Freedoms were by no means American conceptions. They were derived rather from traditions of Western thought and had their roots in idealistic philosophies of other days.

In the years since World War II we have been shifting about, vaguely uncomfortable in not being able to clarify in our own minds the "American character." Publications such as those of the Luce empire have been sounding clarion calls to articulate a "national purpose." [6] The relative failure of these efforts have been noted recently in a number of scholarly discourses.[7] The entire campaign has suffered from one essential paradox: that the richest and most powerful nation in the world, which has gained its success largely without exploitation or oppression of others, feels impelled to *justify* its riches, power, and success. If we had none of these things, we would indeed have a purpose—to achieve them! Having already achieved them, we—like Mr. Luce standing in front of the *Time* and *Life* building—have now to conjure up a *raison d'etre* for this magnificent edifice.

Since we have failed to find anything like a clear sense of national destiny in the years since V-J Day, it is no surprise that the image we project to others is confused, contradictory,

and unsatisfactory. Our present Attorney General, in his pere-
grinations around the globe, was amazed to find how pro-
foundly "misunderstood" we are both by our friends and our
enemies; might have been even more amazed if he had found
us "understood" perfectly abroad, since we do not even seem to
understand ourselves.

So intensive has been this search for national identity that
we have turned to the strangest sources to tell us who we are.
One classic device has been to ask foreigners to tell us, as
though De Crèvecoeur in the eighteenth century and De
Tocqueville and Bryce in the nineteenth, by some psychological alchemy, could have captured a vision of our national life
that we have missed in part because we are too close to ourselves. Max Lerner, in his encyclopedic *America As a Civilization*,[8] relies to an almost unbelievable degree upon foreign
observers for his section on the *idea* of America. Implicit in
the choice of these sources is the notion that we are somehow
more clearly understood by non-Americans than by ourselves.[9]

There is no good reason why Europeans should compre-
hend America and its national purpose better than native observers; on the contrary, there are many reasons why they
should not. The objectivity that may be provided by an outside
vantage ground is inadequate compensation for a view at close
range. That is why foreign critics are prone to clichés, hasty
generalizations, and unqualified reactions to special cases.

What our Attorney General found as he traveled around
the world in April of 1962 was that we were misunderstood
in a manner which caused him deep concern. And if we are
misunderstood, one reason is that the nation admits of such
vast contradictions as to make almost any kind of statement
about it valid in one degree or another.

A remarkable (although unfortunately poorly annotated)
book by Edward W. Chester entitled *Europe Views Amer-*

ica[10] sets itself the task of studying what European intellectuals have thought about America from the period of World War I to the present. Relying heavily upon such critics as Arnold Toynbee, Harold Laski, Denis Brogan, and many others, it presents the main threads of European comment on the American image—and what a series of interesting contradictions emerge! Here is a mélange of propositions culled by Mr. Chester from European sources:

1. There is no such thing as an American; we are a vastly variegated nation.

2. The Americanization of minority groups in the United States has been remarkable.

3. Americans are, nevertheless, youthful, conformist, and bigoted.

4. Political life in America reflects a basic hypocrisy of the American people: while we are extreme political idealists in theory, we often do not practice what we preach.

5. Capitalism has created prosperity for the American worker, but the worker in America is frequently exploited.

6. America is one of the most prosperous nations in the world, but her natural resources are being wasted.

7. America and the USSR are remarkably similar nations.

8. Americans do not take religion as seriously as Europeans do.

9. Americans are materialists and worship "success."

10. Intellectuals do not fare as well in the United States as in Europe.

11. America's main intellectual contributions have been in the field of philosophy and literature.

12. American education is frequently attacked because it is not European.

13. American culture is frequently attacked because it is not truly American.

Generalizations like these are invariably confusing. As Chester points out, however, certain specific sensitive areas of American life seem to be of main concern to the European, namely, our treatment of minority groups (particularly the Negro), our extraordinary national wealth and prosperity, and the state of our intellectual life and popular culture.

Especially revealing, perhaps, is the following quotation from an essay by Mochtar Lubis, an Indonesian newspaperman, author, and anti-Communist. Although he later indicates how his viewpoint about the USA was changed upon further investigation, here are the first impressions of the USA as he saw us. They reveal, of course, a thousand stereotypes of the American image, many of which are believed quite seriously as the sole truth about the United States in many corners of the world. Writes Lubis:

My first weeks of travel tended to confirm my preconceived ideas about the country. And I received another impression: an illusion of uniformity and conformity. I use the word "illusion" for reasons I will make clear later.

America is mechanical, a technical civilization, a gigantic machine monster. Machines, gadgets, buttons to push everywhere, and everywhere, and everywhere. People talk machines, use machines, work machines, control machines, are controlled by machines; already they are planning fully automatic factories where machines will produce machines. An American city is nothing like any other city on earth: the feverish atmosphere, the machines and machines, pushbuttons and pushbuttons, and the terrible haste; people everywhere are in a perpetual hurry; they do not walk but half run.

In traveling from city to city I was haunted by "Come on to my House." The blaring song, crashing through the air night and day, followed me wherever I went (it was the hit of the year). I disliked the song intensely. To me it was cheap, and tended to confirm my preconceived idea of the shallowness of American culture, its materialism, superficiality, uniformity and conformity.

Mass advertisements in newspapers, radio, TV, billboards, for twenty-four hours a day, seven days a week, fifty-two weeks a year, year after year, telling people to go to the same places, buy the same cars, gadgets, dresses, build the same houses, read the same pulp literature, to feel the same, think the same. Through the power of the mass-communications media, the same likes and dislikes, a leveling down of taste, character, personality: uniformity, conformity. The same garish neon signs from city to city. The uniformity of food; the fine art of cooking and eating corrupted by the invention of canned foods. Uniformity even in politics. People told me they always voted Republican or Democratic because they had always done so, because everybody did so—family, friends, city, or state. Everybody likes Eisenhower; "he's a nice guy" was the most frequent reason.

Detroit! The Ford factory. The might of machines, the endless belt of mass production: motorcars, refrigerators, radios, television sets, machines, fountain pens, canned goods—a consumer's society. The kitchen helper at my hotel had his own automobile—incredible! Saw my first automobile graveyard: what a terrible waste. And what sinful waste in restaurants— all the good food that was thrown away.

Shocked to see in the South signs "For Whites Only," "For Colored." In a New Orleans tram I deliberately broke the rule by sitting in the "for colored" section; got the biggest surprise of my life when the conductor apologized and said that I must sit up front. I am brown; I am colored too. These Southern people's fine distinction of color is beyond me! In a nightclub in New Orleans a young Negro girl sang "Too Young to Remember." The guests were mostly whites. The blacks were good enough to entertain the whites and work for them, and no more. A leader of the National Association for the Advancement of Colored People told me in New Orleans that even in churches the Negroes were allowed to sit only in the rear. What an insult to God! Saw advertisements in Negro publications offering special remedies to straighten kinky hair. The whites have succeeded in instilling such a monstrous inferiority complex in the Negro that he is now ashamed of his own hair!

What a sad sight these Indian lands outside Albuquerque in New Mexico: the Indians, the orphans of America, living in orphanages called reservations, sandwiched between their old traditional life and the relentless advance of American modern technology.

Talked with an American about the increasing juvenile delinquency. Horrified to hear his stories about young people taking drugs, committing murders, robberies, assaults. Too much freedom? Parents losing control over their children? [11]

Perspectives like those of Lubis (granting that they were only his first impressions and were subsequently qualified) are not at all uncommon. As one might expect, they are even encouraged in certain places. Anti-American propaganda in the USSR makes much of these themes, as the following news item demonstrates:

Moscow, Sept. 24, 1962—

Mme. Aleksei I. Adzhubei, journalist daughter of Premier Khrushchev, wrote in the magazine *Ogonyok* today that Americans are "infected, poisoned and ruined by the mad pursuit of money."

Commenting on reports of a new more moral code for the United States Government workers, Mme. Adzhubei said it was like giving medicine to a dead man. What is needed, she said, is a complete overhaul of the United States system. It, in itself, breeds crime, she declared.

The moral, from top to bottom, from Washington to the smallest hamlet is: "Grab what you can," she wrote.[12]

Or, as the *New York Times'* Seymour Topping reports, *Pravda* itself delights in turning this face of the United States toward the Russian people. Says Topping:

Here is the picture of United States life that was projected for the Soviet people by their press:

"What has America accomplished as it approaches the start of a new year?" asked *Pravda,* the Communist party newspaper that dilineates the line for all Soviet communications media.

If one should thumb through the latest newspapers and magazines, *Pravda* reported, one will sense a putrid cemetery smell coming from their pages. It seems as though bourgeois morality, the iron law which says man is a wolf to man has exposed itself as never before.

Pravda selected these newspaper stories as representative of United States life:

An interview with a police superintendent who said that more than 1,000 Negroes had been imprisoned because they had demonstrated for equal rights with white people.

A story of a yacht skipper who had murdered his wife and four passengers, including two children, to obtain $100,000 in insurance.

A public discussion on whether a person has the moral right to shoot a neighbor's child who tried to take cover in his bomb shelter.

A beauty contest to select Miss Fall-out.[13]

This is propagands *within* the USSR, but its tone and nature are echoed by Communist propaganda everywhere and significantly color what people overseas think of us, our way of life, and our values. Tragically, all these charges are just true enough to the casual observer to be acceptable by anyone who desires to think the worst of us.[14]

Such criticism, of course, fits neatly into the Soviet "line": that capitalism and its attendant class struggle yield decadence and depravity and that the high degree of material prosperity known by the West is an illusion which covers a deeper barbarism and shallowness. Only the true socialist (really Communist) state can achieve both material prosperity and civilization in its highest sense, so goes the argument.

Raymond Aron, a French sociologist and newspaperman, has divided anti-American attitudes into four categories.[15]

They apply to the attitudes of the French people he has known, but they smell strongly of Moscow's persuasion and are probably—in one or another variation—typical of most foreign hostility to the United States and its rationale. Here they are with slight modification:

1. *Hostility to the "mass" aspect of American society.* This viewpoint is suspicious of mass production, mass consumption, and standardization. It sees the United States as the wellspring of the "revolt of the masses,"* and of the debasement of standards in the interests of the lowest common denominator of satisfactions sought by the Average Man. It stresses the confusion Americans show between the "average" and the "normal." It fears the mass effects of spreading so widely goods and services which are "satisfactory" but do not achieve excellence.

2. *Hostility to the way America handles her race problems.* In this regard it is the distance between what Americans *say* and what they *do* that seems to disturb foreigners. Few nations of the world—including France with her continental Moslem problem—are free of racial or religious bigotry, but, because Americans have held such high ideals of equality and have talked so long and loudly about them, foreigners expect America to be pure and lily-white in these matters. While many foreigners can understand some kinds of prejudice in America (say, religious prejudice), other forms of American bigotry (as in politics or on the matter of skin color) are almost certain to be incomprehensible to them.

3. *Hostility to the impersonality and superficiality of re-*

* The "revolt of the masses" is a concept discussed in the 1920's by the Spanish philosopher José Ortega y Gasset. He based his observations on European societies where old-established traditions of *noblesse oblige* were giving way to an irresponsible preoccupation with momentary satisfactions.

lationships in American life. This viewpoint sees the individual American as immature, jejune, and incapable of feeling the deep ties of love and friendship that adults should experience. No doubt as a result of the adolescence exported by Hollywood films, many foreigners think that shallowness in the American character leads us to a preoccupation with sexuality (as opposed to genuine sensuality and fulfillment), violence, and general irresponsibility. Manifestations of this facet of our culture are visible in the output of our mass communications.

4. *Hostility to American mass culture and the intellectual pap we seem so to relish.* Critics taking this tack see us as childish and silly barbarians. They cite the millions of copies of American scandal magazines, astrology journals, and sensational newspapers, our digest books and self-help publications—even our "great books" courses and efforts at adult education—all of which attempt to simplify the difficult business of education and to distribute a diluted, pre-digested "culture" to the millions.

As Aron notes, these ideas about us are so generalized that they touch many aspects of American life: the way we allow our children to tyrannize over us; the fact that we (not unlike the Soviet Union[16]) live in something like a child-oriented society; our vulgarities and naivetés; and a thousand other behavior traits which to foreigners appear either strange or boorish, and seem to bear out the animadversions of the critics.

An amusing description of just how odd we can appear to others was published in 1962 in an Iranian newspaper. Obviously written by an individual who was thoroughly familiar with American ways, it concerns Americans who are living in the Near East. Because it offers a clear view of

how we look through the eyes of culture foreign to us, it is
quoted here at length:

THE YANKS

Report on "Minorities" in Iran
by Gregory Lima

The Yanks are an English-speaking tribe of nomads who
have relatively recently arrived in large numbers in Iran. They
are for the most part an unassimilated group with a tenacious
hold on their own customs, tribal rites, and distinctive costume.

Theirs is one of the largest migrations to Iran since the
Mongol invasion and the arrival of the Quashghai in Shiraz.
The Quashghai came to Iran from the east, the Yanks from
the west. They are further distinguished from the Quashghai
by having left their horses, sheep, and goats behind them, and
by travelling in aircraft and automobiles rather than by pack
animal. They can also usually be told apart by their customs
of blowing their noses in bits of paper and carrying their provisions in small tin cans.

The Yanks, who apparently in their homeland once fought
a bitter war among themselves, similar to that fought by the
Turcoman Black Sheep and White Sheep, are not all pleased
to be called Yanks. Some would rather be called Rebels. They
were part of a separatist movement some 100 years ago which
was crushed by the central authority.

.   .   .   .

Nevertheless, the two groups get on harmoniously enough,
intermarry when they are of the same colour, and quarrel about
the past normally only under the influence of a form of Arak,
called whiskey, which they import in liberal quantities from
their original homeland.

Tribal Rite
This whiskey is normally served in a tribal rite called the
cocktail party. A cocktail party is a gathering of adults in the

late afternoon, during which no one is allowed to sit down. Each adult holds a glass of cold liquid concocted according to various formulae designed to stimulate the appetite, loosen the tongue, lessen social inhibitions, and create business contacts.

Into each glass may be placed a cherry, an olive, or an onion, but this, it is said, is only to make the drink look pretty. Some of the adults are known to bring the cherries home to the children, concentrating their whole attention on the liquid.

Others, who normally have not told their children where they are going, have given up the pretense of fruit and vegetables in their glasses, and ask for plain whiskey on rocks. The rocks luckily are soluble and very few people have been known to choke on them.

On such occasions it is usual for such people who have swallowed too many rocks to swear they will never go to another cocktail party again. But tribal custom demands their participation, and the rite continues, sometimes with extraordinary frequency in the course of any single week. Business, properly cemented, goes on as usual.

But if there are obviously no cocktails in a cocktail, there is also no ham in a hamburger. Nor is there dog in a hot dog, although in Iran it is sometimes suggested that there might be. This makes the language of the Yanks somewhat difficult, and leads to a tendency not to believe everything they say. Which is unfortunate. They are usually very sincere people.

Backward

But they are somewhat backward. Though they have settled largely in the cities in Iran, notably Tehran, their habits are not fully urban. They have difficulty crossing the streets as pedestrians, and even greater trouble handling an automobile in traffic as drivers. As drivers they have a tendency to stop at red lights, holding up all the other cars behind them. They also have a tendency to signal a left turn when they actually wish to go to the left. This frequently causes considerable confusion.

.   .   .   .

Mating

They also have peculiar mating habits. The men never hold hands with men. They hold hands with women. Men rarely kiss each other in public, and when they do, they receive peculiar looks. But men kiss women in public. This, however, does not lead to early marriage.

It leads to a type of courtship called petting, which, like suburban living, is neither quite here or there. Sometimes, however, it does get there. They get married. They ultimately raise what are called teenagers.

Teenagers are a separate sub-tribe in themselves. They have their own rituals, customs and language. Sometimes the language approximates English. But those words are not used too often. Most teenagers learn English as a second language at school. One of the peculiarities of their accent may derive from a mouth full of chewing gum. It whitens teeth and defects speech. It is the teenager's latter-day substitute for thumbsucking.

.　　.　　.　　.　　.　　.　　.　　.　　.

The amount of information they absorb between comic books, late night television serials, and writing fan letters to Elvis Presley is astounding. They are a people with extraordinary enthusiasm for the trivia of life, with enough energy left over to distinguish themselves in science, business, and the arts—which never ceases to amaze the parents of each succession of teenagers. This is to say nothing of the amazement shown in the countries to which these nomads migrate with their teenagers.

Hygienic

They are a hygienic people. They add chlorine to water like other tribesmen add salt to their food. And although they may throw empty beer cans in their swimming pools, they bathe frequently. They do so as at cocktail parties—standing up. The water comes from a sprinkler over their heads. They don't lie down as in a proper *haman,* pour water on themselves from a pan, or scrub themselves with pumice stone. They turn this sprinkler on full force, and like instant coffee, they just add water to soap, without percolating or wasting time soaking.

.   .   .   .

He has so many gadgets that he lives in a world apart. He lives in a different temperature, eats different food, seeks different recreation. He loses his individulaity and becomes a type. People know more about him from the cinema than they do in actual life. He is two parts Gary Cooper and one part hero. That is to say, when things are going well. Otherwise, he becomes two parts Jerry Lewis and one part Boris Karloff.

Maybe they will be better understood when more of the other tribes keep their provisions in little tin cans, give up their pack donkeys for automobiles, live in suburban villas with swimming pools for water holes, and give birth, not in the ordinary way, to children, but to teenagers. It seems perfectly obvious that if all the other tribes had teenagers the Yanks would be more easily understood.[17]

Most curious to foreigners and the best grist for the mill of Soviet propaganda is the discovery that the land of milk and honey still manifests rampant poverty, slums, and migrant "wetbacks." Non-Americans are amazed at the hundreds of social abuses which a society as rich as America (and as proud of its "know-how") seems unable to prevent, while nations like Denmark and Sweden have, in large measure, found a way to ameliorate them.[18] We make no secret of these bleak facts in our literature, and writers like Nelson Algren, John Steinbeck, and Erskine Caldwell have been instrumental in spreading the image of this America far and wide. The foreign reader is not interested in a sophisticated economic rationale; the picture of distress and hardship, even if overdrawn for dramatic effect, simply does not make sense in the light of over-all American affluence. And must we not ruefully acknowledge that he is basically right?

He looks not only at the way in which our massive economy is distributed, but also at the way we allocate our loyalties, our adulations, and our laurels. He observes that many of us esteem movie stars more than poets, baseball players more than professors, popular singers more than serious composers; and he scratches his head in wonderment at what manner of man the American is, despite the fact that his own country probably has not wholly eschewed the pursuit of shoddy values.

The proclivity in the USA to exalt the trivial also puzzles literary critic J. Donald Adams, who is an American but whose words might be heard from the lips of millions of non-Americans observing the way we distribute the prizes of life. He writes:

> What about our enthronement of personality?
> What is the significance of this mounting obsession, so evident in most of the magazines of huge circulation? Why do we give such exaggerated attention to singers who cannot sing, comedians who are not comic, exhibitionists who have nothing to exhibit? Why are the names of great engineers, great teachers, great physicians unknown to the general public? What is so important about the financial size of the contract which this baseball player or that football coach has just signed? Is it interest in art or amazement that more than two million dollars should be paid for a painting, so that unprecedented thousands go to gape at a Rembrandt in the Metropolitan Museum? Why do millions feel drunk with power at the wheel of an automobile? There are many more such questions.[19]

These are good questions which reflect a weakness in American culture, no worse than many comparable aspects of life in foreign lands, but well-exploited by our enemies.

In the absence of any other image of America, we sometimes unwittingly present at first glance a picture of a smug, stupid, childish, overfed, vulgar, irresponsible people—and nothing more. This is not, however, the America in which the authors of this book live, and it is not the one inhabited by you, the reader. Of course it is a side of America which most certainly exists, and unfortunately it gives rise to an image which is readily exportable because it is so obvious—so close to the surface of our national ilfe.

But what about other images? Is it possible to do what our publishers, editors, movie-makers, TV producers, and others have thus far failed to do: articulate a worthwhile national character for America and substitute for an easy image one of greater depth and greater relevance to the goals and values of civilized people in other lands? Unquestionably it is, but before we try we must discover why, up to now, most attempts to convince others of the serious qualities of our ethos have bogged down.

The answer is that we have done too much talking and not enough listening. Most of what we have said in the past and much of what we say today is scoffed at and disbelieved simply because the United States has assumed the stance of a nation that is ever ready to tell others what to do but pays no heed to the wisdom which others have to offer it.

In short, our parochialism has been self-defeating. We have been and are ready to teach the world the democratic way of life, export our material excellence, our "know-how," our values, our morals, our culture, our system of education, our frozen foods, our philosophers, our tourists, some of our atomic secrets—almost anything and everything that we think will buy for us the love of people abroad.

But people in foreign lands do not want to sell us their love. They want us to respect them, and would respect us in turn if we permitted them to do so. They are ready to *trade* with us, not only in terms of economics, but in terms of cultural and intellectual exchange. Nations, being composed of human beings, like to be appreciated; to brush them aside, to see nothing of significance in their daily lives, is to offer them a gratuitous affront.

A writer from Turkey puts the problem in these simple terms:

> More serious than indequate knowledge of a fact about foreign countries is, I think, a certain failure to understand the psychology of foreign nations. Many Americans, I have found, easily assume that all peoples have the same standards and attitudes as they. Thus America was very slow in detecting the Machiavellian element in the policy of some countries with which she came into close contact, an element that her own policy has generally lacked. Americans appear particularly to overlook the weight of irrational and emotional motivations in the conduct of some foreign nations, and to incline to think that difficulties can generally be overcome by material means. Insufficient comprehension of the often dissimilar mentality of foreign peoples has, I think, occasionally led to mistakes in policy and to bad feelings in personal contacts.[20]

The average Turk, he goes on to say, "has probably come to know more about America than the average American knows of Turkey." Such one-sidedness cannot help but be conducive to a feeling that America is just "not interested" in those intangible qualities which a country like Turkey, with its durable traditions, has to offer the New World. An indifferent America, to the Turk, seems accordingly to be a not-so-beautiful America.

When it is put another way by a Yugoslavian observer, Marija Vilfan, one can almost hear the resentment seethe beneath the following statement:

> In the field of cultural exchange the picture is as follows. Since the war hundreds of American novels, short stories, and other books have been translated into Yugoslav languages. Many American plays are in the repertory of our theaters.

Yugoslav music lovers have heard Stokowski, the Minneapolis Symphony Orchestra, have seen *Porgy and Bess,* the New York Ballet Theater. We have seen among others the exhibition of Contemporary American Plastic Arts, that of contemporary American lithographs, prepared by the Cincinnati Art Museum, the photograph exhibition, "Family of Man," which pleased us very much. A great many American films are being shown in Yugoslavia, and US papers and books are sold freely.

But US-Yugoslav cultural exchanges are one-track. No work of Yugoslav literature has been translated in America. Only the Janigro Zagreb chamber-music orchestra and two folk-dance groups have given successful recitals. There are no exhibitions of our painters and sculptors. While American exhibitions in Yugoslavia are being organized with at least partial state assistance, US official circles have never extended an invitation or offered their assistance for the organization of Yugoslav cultural activities in the US; apart from the interest of private US citizens, this is left entirely to commercial channels. In the case of small nations reciprocity in cultural exchanges cannot be achieved through the initiative of private managers. I think the US government should help in promoting exchanges and acquainting its citizens with foreign cultures—which is already the usual practice in Europe.[21]

Such cultural exchanges have occurred in recent years but, by and large, the rank and file of *our* citizens have not been exposed to them. True, Russian dancers have appeared for a few moments on Ed Sullivan's TV show and in films; yet, for all practical purposes, our three major TV networks remain deaf, dumb, and blind to the vast resources of drama, dance, music, and talent of many kinds that can help to interpret to the American citizen the aspirations and values of other nations. Perhaps following the advent of Telstar in July, 1962, we may see, not only a new era of international television, but increasing prospects of mutual international understanding.

Cultural exchanges with Iron Curtain nations pose a neat problem for America. They are not without their risks because Communist nations have a way of squeezing every possible advantage out of them for their side on the cold war, or else they refuse to go along with the idea in the first place. A sizeable school of thought, justifiably, is of the opinion that Americans are usually left holding the bag in the matter of cultural exchange. While this risk is ever present, and we should certainly be aware of it, there is no reason why Communist countries should necessarily be able to take advantage of our willingness to listen to what they have to say, *if* our guard is up and *if* we judge their motives correctly. Also, if the exchanges are *quid pro quo,* with the United States putting its best foot forward, there is no good reason why *our* idea invaders should not make a better impression in Iron Curtain countries than their propagandists make on us.

Most Americans immerse themselves in local radio and newspapers, national television programs, and Hollywood movies, and leave to a select élite the pitifully few cultural and educational offerings which many nations of the world would be more than happy to see broadcast to our citizens via our mass media of communications.

What we are proposing is simply this: If the "image" of America is to be improved in the minds eyes of the millions upon millions of people overseas who think ill of us at present, we must, as a nation, take notice of the attitudes of these millions and listen to them with a sympathetic ear. And we must let them know we are listening and that we *care.* This should be done in an organized and methodical manner.

The United States needs an *Ear of America*—a governmental or private agency which will match, if not in resources at least in missionary zeal and breadth of operation, the effort that the current voices of America put forth. Its aim should be the importation from abroad of all that is worth-while in foreign culture, education, and political life in order to reactivate the sort of fruitfulness and creativity yielded by the old American Melting Pot. Better yet, a symphony of world culture would emerge, which would bring about a new American idealism and even, God save the mark, a rein-vigorated patriotism.

Conservatives may yell "Globaloney," super-patriots may wave the flag as they denounce "subversion," and certain Southern and Midwestern Senators may regard the leavening of our culture as the work of the devil himself. Actually, not all of these protests would be chimerical; we cannot afford to jeopardize what is uniquely fine and valuable in American society, and conservatism would exercise its rightful function of guarding against dilution of solid national qualities.

But an Ear of America we must nevertheless create, not with the purpose of asking non-Americans to define the "American character" or lecture us on our imperialism, ma-terialism, and mass culture, but in order to have a reference point from which we will be able to see more clearly our own virtues—and weaknesses. Since, at present, we have so feeble an understanding of other ways of life, our efforts at com-prehending our own lack the world perspective which alone could bring them into proper focus. We do not need to be told who we are. This we must discover for ourselves, *in the light of what we discover about others*, at whatever risks we run of misunderstanding those others.

The popular pollsters tell us that isolationism is dead, that it is no longer a viable political or diplomatic philosophy. It is, however, merely physical isolationism which is no longer possible in this age of jet planes, rockets, and express com-munications; isolationism of the mind is still very much alive and its delusory quality is just as dangerous as the ostrich-like posture of generations past.

The truth is that Wendell Willkie's old ideal of One World has been achieved, but not on the territorial basis which he emphasized. The terrors that now threaten every human being on the face of the globe mean that *we are all in it together*. People everywhere stand mutually engaged, whether they like it or not, in a common fate. None is or can ever again be isolated from the other by anything except ignorance, apathy, or sloth. Psychological isolationism is no more tenable in the second half of the twentieth century than the belief that toads cause warts or that alchemy is a science.

To a disturbing degree, however, Americans are still psychologically isolated from the rest of the world. They are a people frantically searching to discover their identities, their purposes, and the mainsprings of their national genius. They are unbelievably given to the contemplation of their navels, simply because they are divorced from the realities of a world which vainly looks to them for leadership.

Of course they don't know who they are or what their purpose is. One can achieve identity only in company with others. The American people have allowed their mass media, their culture, and their national life—political, social, and economic—to offer them nothing but the smallest and shallowest part of a rich potential. They have excluded all strange or unwelcome voices, with the result that psychological isolationism has today reached epidemic proportions.

On the other hand, they are a people fantastically generous in their gifts and assistance to the rest of the world. They are an open, warm, companionable people. Tense and restless, independent and freedom-loving, they are a people formed in the crucible of revolution and still capable of expressing the dynamism implicit in their roots. They are a complex amalgam of separate and heterogeneous cultures that far transcend the stereotypes of Hollywood and television. They support a vast wealth of private and public theaters, libraries, symphonies, art galleries, operatic and ballet companies, schools and colleges, and every other kind of cultural endeavor. They are a resourceful people. They are a creative people.

As for an Ear of America! If we listen to other voices, see other images, and grow to love what is good while rejecting what is bad in foreign insights into human society and the human condition, we shall discover quickly who we are and what our aims and goals must be for the second half of the present century.

Let us devote a part of our wealth, as never before, to turning our educational system, radio, television, magazines, and newspapers into "windows on the world." In the following paragraphs Adlai Stevenson speaks about education, but his remarks go far beyond a concern for formal schooling; they outline an "education for life" that is a necessity today for every American. Wrote Stevenson:

> We hear about "adjusting to life." Of course, but what is life today? If this means a child's learning to live easily with the members of his family and the rest of the people in the block, fitting smoothly into his environment in his church, feeling at ease with the people he sees from day to day, then I think we have drawn in the circle dangerously small. For distance and time and space have shrunk; "life" is never again going to be a local island for any man or woman in the world.
>
> Looking ahead for the long pull—not just to missiles and rockets—the American problem in education is to prepare citizens not merely to live in American society, but to live in an America caught up inextricably in an evolving world community, which, in turn, is seized by both technological and political revolution.
>
> This means new dimensions for education. It means the

training of innovators, not organization men, in both science and humanities. It means the understanding of other societies. And it means a deeper understanding of American history and society, not merely as a unique and treasured saga, but as part of universal experience. Instinctive knowledge of the round of American life as it is lived at home is not enough.

Yes, adjust children to life—to life in the world in which they live—a world where, among other things, the vast majority who are not white, the vast majority who are uneducated, are now demanding their birthrights as children equal in the sight of God.[22]

We had better listen to these voices while there is still time. They will not speak long unless they know that America is really listening to them. It is time we perked up our ears.

How is this for an American "purpose?" It is the destiny of America to stop, look, listen, and learn, to the end of achieving a truly wise and humane nation, dedicated to the cultivation of freedom, civic virtue, and equal opportunity for all. The America of tomorrow will then be a country where all the best that man has created in his diversity of cultures will be apportioned equitably on the basis of what Jefferson called "natural talent."

In simple terms, it will be our purpose to *improve*.

We have a long way to go. Idea invaders all over the world are begging for attention. Let's listen to them. And *evaluate* the ideas!

POSTSCRIPT

The world-wide communication of ideas will come most potently by means of an honest break-through between man and man as *individuals,* and hence between nation and nation. We may expect this millennium when mankind gives up convenient generalizations, neat classifications, and pretentious concepts like "images" and "posturings," employed by propaganda professionals in arriving at sometimes confusing and inaccurate conclusions. Today, we all need desperately the invasion of objective self-truths.

NOTES

CHAPTER 1

[1] William Albig, *Modern Public Opinion,* New York: McGraw-Hill Book Co., Inc., 1956, pp. 293-295.

[2] Norman Foerster (ed.), *American Poetry and Prose,* New York: Houghton Mifflin Co., 1947, p. 196.

[3] L. John Martin, *International Propaganda,* Minneapolis: University of Minnesota Press, 1958, pp. 5-6.

[4] Albig, *op. cit.,* p. 293.

[5] See Christian Gauss's excellent introduction in Niccolo Machiavelli, *The Prince,* New York: Mentor Books, 1961, pp. 1-32, upon which much of the following was based. A study of *The Prince* is, of course, valuable for all students of modern propaganda.

[6] Machiavelli, *op. cit.,* p. 15-16.

[7] The following material can be found in part in Bertrand Russell, *Wisdom of the West,* New York: Doubleday and Co., 1959, pp. 180-181.

[8] The whole story of this fabrication is nowhere more amusingly told than in Josephine Tey's mystery story *The Daughter of Time,* New York: Berkeley Publishing Corp., New York, 1960. Tey even attempts to find out who really murdered the children!

[9] Gustave Le Bon, *The Crowd,* New York: The Viking Press, 1960.

[10] L. John Martin, *op. cit.,* pp. 7-9.

CHAPTER 2

[1] For confirmation of this bit of bad news, see G. M. Gilbert, *Nuremberg Diary,* New York: Signet Books, 1961, pp. 33-35. Gilbert, a psychologist had the doubtful pleasure of measuring the intelligence of 21 top Nazis at the time of the War Crimes Trials (Goebbels not among them, of course). Not one of them—even Hess who was in a psychotic state—had intelligence below the average for the population, and nine of them scored between 130 and 143 on conventional intelligence tests.

[2] Eric Hoffer, *The True Believer,* New York: Mentor Books, 1958.

[3] Louis P. Lochner, *The Goebbels Diaries,* New York: Doubleday and Co., 1948, p. 476.

[4] William L. Shirer, *The Rise and Fall of the Third Reich,* New York: Simon and Schuster, 1960. Material in the section to follow was based largely on pp. 241-256. Specific citations will not be given, except to quotations.

[5] Lochner, *op. cit.,* p. 13.

[6] Shirer, *op. cit.,* p. 241.

[7] The organizational chart for the Ministry appears in Roger Manvell and Heinrich Fraenkel, *Dr. Goebbels,* New York: Pyramid Books, 1961, p. 131.

[8] Lochner, *op. cit.,* p. 56.

[9] Manvell and Fraenkel, *op. cit.,* p. 193.

[10] *Ibid,* p. 195.

[11] Manvell and Fraenkel, *op. cit.,* p. 139. Much of the material in the paragraphs is taken from pp. 140-141.

[12] Curt Riess, *Joseph Goebbels,* New York: Ballantine Books, 1960, pp. 105-106.

[13] The material that follows is largely taken from O. John Rogge,

The Official German Report, New York: Thomas Yoseloff, 1961. The pages condensed here are pp. 44ff., 64ff., 305ff. Only direct quotations will be cited individually in the section that follows.

14 *Ibid.,* pp. 44-45.

15 See Jerome S. Bruner's excellent study in Daniel Katz, *et al.,* *Public Opinion and Propaganda,* New York: The Dryden Press, 1954, pp. 491-506, the source of much of the material which appears here.

16 *Ibid.,* p. 494.

17 *Ibid.,* p. 495.

18 W. E. Daugherty and M. Janowitz, *A Psychological Warfare Casebook,* Baltimore: The Johns Hopkins Press, 1958, pp. 235-237 for an excellent outline of Joyce's strange career.

19 Rogge, *op. cit.,* pp. 310-319.

20 *Ibid.,* pp. 305-306. Analysis of many of these broadcasts can be found in Alexander L. George, *Propaganda Analysis,* Evanston, Ill.: Row, Peterson and Co., 1959, an interesting book which, unfortunately, demonstrates the social scientists' love of devising analytic methods so complex that they miss the point of what they are dissecting and obscure the obvious.

21 Rogge, *op. cit.,* pp. 64-66.

22 *Ibid.,* p. 65.

CHAPTER 3

1 Alex Inkles, *Public Opinion in Soviet Russia,* Cambridge: The Harvard University Press, 1958, pp. 17, 21-22.

2 Congress of the United States, *The Technique of Soviet Propaganda,* Washington: Government Printing Office, 1960 (86th Congress, 2nd Session) p. III. The estimate is made by Senator Eastland.

3 Donald Dunham, *Kremlin Target U.S.A.,* New York: Ives Washburn, Inc., 1961, p. 7.

[4] L. John Martin, *International Propaganda,* Minneapolis: The University of Minnesota Press, 1958, pp. 46-54.

[5] The authors are indebted to Alfred Berzins of the *Crusade for Freedom* for his insights into Soviet persuasion which he so freely shared with them. Mr. Berzins has had first-hand experience with skilled Communist propagandists of various kinds.

[6] Berzins' book, *The Unpublished Crime,* New York: Speller and Sons, 1962, contains detailed examples of these efforts as well as an accurate record of how Soviet propaganda and agitation were used to conquer Latvia, Mr. Berzins' native country.

[7] First-hand examination of these propaganda devices and personal experience with "public relations" officers at the Soviet Legation in New York City has been augmented by careful reference to the excellent section in Dunham, *op. cit.,* pp. 84-86, and the other following citations from this book.

[8] *Ibid,* pp. 247-249.

[9] Congress of the U.S., *op. cit.,* pp. 23-28, revised slightly.

[10] Dunham, *op. cit.,* pp. 215-216.

CHAPTER 4

[1] Max Lerner, *America as a Civilization,* New York: Simon and Schuster, 1957, p. 929.

[2] *USSR Magazine,* November, 1959.

[3] The following has been based mostly on Alex Inkeles and Raymond A. Bower, *The Soviet Citizen,* Cambridge, Mass: The Harvard University Press, 1959, pp. 189-230.

[4] *USSR,* loc. cit.

[5] *The New York Times,* September 20, 1959.

[6] The following material was taken largely from *The New York Times,* September 20, 21 and 22, 1959.

[7] *Time Magazine,* September 28, 1959, pp. 15-16.

[8] *Loc. cit.*

[9] *The New York Times,* September 20, 1959.

[10] *Loc. cit.*

[11] Text of speech by Premier Khrushchev at Municipal Dinner held in Los Angeles and reprinted in *The New York Times,* September 21, 1959. (Italics supplied).

[12] Summary of the Dinner Debate between U.S. Union leaders and Khrushchev printed in *The New York Times,* September 22, 1959, p. 20. (Italics supplied).

[13] *The New York Times,* September 21, 1959, p. 17.

[14] Ezra Goodman, *The Fifty Year Decline and Fall of Hollywood,* New York: Simon and Schuster, 1961, pp. 408-410.

[15] *Face to Face With America,* Moscow, 1960, p. 228.

[16] Reprinted in *The New York Times,* September 21, 1959.

[17] The authors wish to thank Lillian Heydorn for her research which validates these conclusions.

CHAPTER 5

[1] U.S. Government Printing Office, 85th Congress, 2nd session, House Document no. 381, *A Report on the Barriers to International Travel,* etc., Washington: 1958, pp. ix-52.

[2] *Ibid,* p. 5.

[3] S. I. Hayakawa, Professor of Language Arts at San Francisco State College, "Formula for Peace: Listening," *The New York Times Magazine,* July 31, 1960, pp. 10, 12.

[4] *Saturday Review,* January 9, 1960, pp. 25-26, 55-59.

[5] *The New York Times Magazine,* March 5, 1961, p. 96.

[6] Statistics employed for the following analysis appear in *Travel News,* April, May and June, 1960 (reprinted by the American Society of Travel Agents, 501 Fifth Avenue, New York 17, New York, p. 13 in the reprint) and in *Profile of the American Tourist,* 1960-61 edition, published by the American Automobile Association, Washington 6, D.C., pp. 24-28. The figures upon which it is based represent statistics given for both the year 1959 and estimates for 1960.

[7] *Saturday Review, op. cit.,* p. 26.

[8] A good example is the article by Robert Coughlan, "How We

Appear to Others," *Life Magazine,* December 23, 1957 pp. 150-152, 154 upon which some of the material which follows is based. Another more positive article is "A Traveler's Credo," *Glamour Magazine,* May, 1960, pp. 130-131, 142, 181.

[9] A good defense can be found in the article by Joan M. Cook, "A Kind Word for Americans on Tour," *The New York Times Magazine,* August 27, 1961, pp. 52, 56, 59 which has been used in the preparation of the following pages.

[10] See *Marketing the United States as a Tourist Destination,* Department of Commerce: Washington D.C., March 1961, pp. 1-50, and *Time Magazine,* December 19, 1960, pp. 31-32 for a more detailed analysis of these problems.

[11] The quotes below are taken from *Marketing the United States, op. cit.,* pp. 15-16.

[12] *American Students Abroad: Goodwill Ambassadors?* The Maxwell Graduate School of Citizenship and Public Affairs, Syracuse University, Jan. 28, 1958, pp. 1-8.

[13] Consult *Time Magazine,* December 5, 1960, for as neat a statement of the "shocking" revolutions of the life of the American Army sybarite as they appeared at the time.

[14] *Life Magazine, op. cit.,* 152, 154, has been largely the source of the comments that follow. They are offered with reservations. The conclusion therein, however, seems to concur with the observations of travel experts with whom this matter has been discussed.

[15] See *The New York Times,* Sunday, September 17, 1961, for Max Frankel's analysis of these exchanges related to the international situation at the time.

[16] *Washington Post and Times Herald,* May 7, 1961.

[17] The authors wish to thank Miss Jeanne Bartolomei who has made an extensive study of the AMREPCO tour and whose research and conclusions have been helpful to them.

[18] *Report of the Committee on Foreign Relations,* United States Senate, 87th Congress, Report No. 372.

[19] *The New York Times,* April 6, 1962.

[20] *Report, op. cit.*, p. 1.

[21] *Yank Magazine,* Special 1960 Issue.

CHAPTER 6

[1] Speech delivered to the leaders of the film industry, November 5, 1961: United States Information Agency, Release No. 48.

[2] Works conjecturing on this state of affairs and the pernicious tendencies of the movies in terms of our foreign relations would be too lengthy to list here. The interested reader might sample William Lynch, *The Image Industries,* New York: Sheed and Ward, 1959; Leo Rosten, *Hollywood,* New York: Harcourt Brace, Co., 1941, and Gilbert Seldes, *The Movies Come From America,* London, Chas. Scribner's Sons, 1937, for some of this discussion.

[3] Robert Knopp, "How We Look To Latin America," *America,* March 7, 1959, pp. 662-664.

[4] *Ibid.,* p. 662.

[5] *Ibid.,* pp. 663-4.

[6] The following information was graciously supplied by Michael Linden, Director of Research of the Motion Picture Association of America, 28 West 44th Street. New York, N. Y.

[7] The problem of the popularity of American films in England is a good example of the loyalty of foreigners to American movies. It is discussed in Roger Manvell's *The Film and the Public,* Harmondsworth, Middlesex, England: Penguin Books, pp. 208-215.

[8] *Basic Facts and Figures,* UNESCO, Geneva, Switzerland, 1959, p. 113.

[9] "East Goes West," *Esquire,* August, 1961, pp. 91-97.

[10] An interesting discussion of Hollywood values appears in Gilbert Seldes, *The Great Audience,* New York: The Viking Press, 1950, pp. 64-87, which treats the role of the Hollywood's production code in enforcing these values.

[11] From *What They Say About Us,* New York: The MPAA, 1961,

p. 2. (mimeographed pamphlet). Any edition from 1958 on will yield the same harvest.

[12] USIA, *op. cit.*, excerpted pp. 1-11 by the authors.

[13] *The New York Times,* Nov. 12, 1961.

[14] *The New York Times,* Dec. 10, 1961.

[15] *Loc. cit.*

[16] Reported in "The Press and America's 'Image' Abroad—An Official Criticism," *U.S. News and World Report,* Dec. 5, 1960, pp. 128-131.

[17] *Ibid.,* pp. 129-130.

[18] A brief overview of this picture can be found in Charles S. Steinberg, *The Mass Communicators,* New York: Harper and Bros., 1958, pp. 175-182.

[19] John Tebbel, "The New York Times Goes West," *Saturday Review,* Nov. 11, 1961, pp. 69-71.

[20] Statistics here are for 1960 and have been rounded off to provide approximations. They come from *Foreign Circulation of Representative US Publications,* 1960, compiled by the Magazine Publisher's Assn., NYC, May 1961, to whom the writers are grateful for their help.

[21] *Publishers' Weekly,* May 22, 1961, pp. 44-45.

[22] *The New York Times,* October 8, 1961.

[23] Other organizations which send books overseas are the International Cooperation Administration, the Asia Foundation, and the Franklin Publications, Inc. (a non-profit translation enterprise.) See *National Book Committee Quarterly,* Fall-Winter, 1961, Information was kindly provided by this organization.

[24] These figures have been taken from *Television* magazine, December, 1961, pp. 58-63, 84-101, as are most of the other statistics which follow.

[25] Robert Lewis Shayon "Breakthrough in International TV," *Saturday Review,* Jan. 14, 1961, pp. 35-47.

[26] "World Laps Up US TV Fare," *Business Week,* April 23, 1960, pp. 129-131.

[27] *Shayon, loc. cit.*

CHAPTER 7

[1] Thomas Aitken, Jr., *A Foreign Policy for American Business,* New York: Harper and Bros., 1962, p. 19.

[2] U.S. Department of Commerce, Report No. FT 140, *United States Exports of Domestic and Foreign Merchandise,* Washington, U.S. Government Printing Office, 1961, Part I, pp. 1-196; Part II, pp. 1-340.

[3] *Newsweek,* Nov. 16, 1959, p. 83.

[4] *Time Magazine,* Feb. 29, 1960, p. 108.

[5] *Business Week,* Oct. 8, 1960, p. 158.

[6] Taken from chart in Aitken, *op. cit.,* pp. 150-152.

[7] *Ibid.,* p. 154.

[8] *Business Week,* Oct. 8, 1960, p. 158.

[9] *Time Magazine,* Nov. 16, 1959, p. 105 and *News Front,* January, 1962, p. 34 contain a description of these supermarkets.

[10] *New York Times,* Feb. 25, 1962.

[11] *Business Week,* April 23, 1960, pp. 124-127.

[12] *Fortune Magazine,* Jan. 1961, p. 83 and *U.S. News and World Report,* Dec. 12, 1960, pp. 70-71.

[13] Speech delivered to the International Executives Assn., Inc., November 14, 1961 (mimeographed copy), p. 6.

[14] *The New York Times,* Jan. 12, 1962.

[15] See the *National Guardian,* Jan. 15, 1962, pp. 6-7, for one viewpoint of labor interests on American business overseas.

[16] *The New York Times,* Feb. 9, 1962.

[17] *New York Times,* Feb. 21, 1962.

[18] Aitken, *op. cit.,* pp. 13-24.

[19] *Ibid.,* p. 142.

[20] *Ibid.,* pp. 144-145.

[21] The brilliant French film "The Wages of Fear" caught some of this hostility at the grassroots level neatly and artistically. It is unfortunate that various scenes delineating this anti-Americanism

in South America were deleted before the movie was shown in the United States. Americans need to be reminded that we are not necessarily beloved even in nations which are highly dependent on us or close to us geographically.

22 Robert L. Heilbroner, *The Worldly Philosophers,* New York: *Time,* Incorporated, 1962 edition, p. 209.

23 Much information about Trade Fairs has been taken from the article "The USA Goes to the Fair," by J. D. Ratcliff in Urban G. Whitaker Jr. *Propaganda and International Relations,* San Francisco, Chandler Publishing Co., 1960, pp. 29-33.

24 See schedule of International Trade Fairs, published yearly by the U.S. Department of Commerce.

25 *The New York Times Magazine,* Jan. 2, 1962, pp. 12, 52.

26 Much of the material in the following paragraphs is based upon two excellent and scholarly articles written, incidentally, for high school children, in *Scholastic Magazine,* February 6, 1959, pp. 8-11. Their clarity and accuracy might be studied with profit by other reporters of the international economic scene, particularly those who think they are writing for adults.

27 *The New York Times,* Jan. 9, 1962.

28 *ICA and US Voluntary Agencies;* Washington, D.C.: Voluntary Foreign Aid Staff: International Cooperation Administration, 1959, pp. 1-22.

29 *Food For Peace,* No. 595047, U.S. Government Printing Office, Washington, D.C., 1961, pp. not numbered.

30 *The New York Times,* March 13, 1962, pp. 1-12 and March 14, 1962.

31 *The New York Times,* March 13, 1962, Editorial.

CHAPTER 8

1 For a detailed history of RFE, see: Robert T. Holt, *Radio Free Europe,* Minneapolis: University of Minnesota Press, 1958, pp. xii-249. Use has been made of this volume in the following section in so free a manner that only major references to the book

will be cited. Other information about RFE was kindly provided by Alton Kastner, Director of Public Information, Free Europe Committee, 2 Park Avenue, New York 16, N.Y., to whom the authors are grateful.

2 The following specifics were drawn, in large part, from the Crusade for Freedom's *Annual Report*, read in galley proof at the time of writing, Spring, 1962. For this reason, page citations cannot be given. Where specific RFE documents are used to augment this information they will be cited.

3 From a mimeographed biography published by the Free Europe Committee.

4 See *The Radio Free Europe Story*, published by the Free Europe Committee, Inc.

5 See the discussion of policy in Holt, *op. cit.*, pp. 57-66.

6 *Annual Report, op. cit.*, pp. not numbered.

7 *The Radio Free Europe Story, op. cit.*, p. 2.

8 This discussion of RFE's programs is based upon Holt, *op. cit.*, pp. 78-103.

9 *Annual Report, op. cit.*, pages not numbered.

10 See *The Press Looks at the Hungarian Revolution*, New York: RFE, no date, no pages.

11 *The Boston Herald*, December 27, 1956.

12 James A. Michener, *The Bridge at Andau*, New York: Random House, 1957, p. 252.

13 Holt, *op. cit.*, p. 142-43.

14 *The New York Times*, January 26, 1957.

15 Mimeographed report of the Council of Europe Special Committee, pp. 1-10.

16 Quoted in *ibid.*, p. 6.

17 Holt, *op. cit.*, p. 212.

18 *The National Guardian*, January 14, 1961, p. 18.

19 *Newsweek*, December 28, 1959, p. 27.

20 Information about Radio Liberty, was obtained from the RL pamphlet *The Most Important Job In the World* and from interviews with Mr. Townsend and Dr. Isaiah Bard of that organization to whom the writers are grateful. See also RL's reprint of

Enno Hobbing's article "The Radio That Speaks for the Silent" in *The Reader's Digest,* November 1958.

[21] Reprinted from a descriptive brochure of the Institute for the Study of the USSR, Manhardstrasse 6, Munich 22, Germany, New York Office: 30 East 42nd Street, N.Y. 17, N.Y.

[22] Institute for the Study of USSR, *Anatomy of Soviet Communism,* pp. 1-56. The programs were produced and narrated by Robert C. Cody and written by Dr. Isaiah Bard. Copies can be obtained at the above address.

[23] *The Saturday Review,* February 11, 1961, p. 85.

CHAPTER 9

[1] Wilson P. Dizard, *Strategy of Truth,* Washington: Public Affairs Press, 1961, p. 187.

[2] *Bulletin* of the Dept. of State, Feb. 6, 1961, p. 185.

[3] Earnest W. Lefever, *Ethics and United States Foreign Policy,* New York: Meridian Books, 1957, pp. 63, 72.

[4] Note must be given here to William P. Dizard's excellent book on the USIA cited above. While much of the material in this chapter was derived from a plethora of documents kindly provided the authors by the USIA itself, Dizard's book is a superbly written history of the Agency, colorful and authoritative, to which students of American international persuasion are recommended. What use we will make of it here will be cited below.

[5] *The Agency in Brief,* Washington: The United States Information Agency, January, 1962, p. B-1. Since this document will be cited so frequently in this chapter, it will be abbreviated below as *Agency.* See also Dizard, *op. cit.,* 29-47 and Edward Barrett, *Truth is Our Weapon,* New York: Funk and Wagnalls Co., 1953, pp. 21-50 for a history of American official propaganda.

[6] *Dizard, op. cit.,* p. 33.

[7] *Ibid.,* pp. 33-37. Also *Agency op. cit.,* pp. B-1, B-2.

[8] *Ibid.,* pp. 39-47.

[9] *Agency, op. cit.,* p. B-4.

[10] *Ibid.,* C-1, E-7.

[11] *Newsweek,* Sept. 18, 1961.

[12] Dizard, *op. cit.,* p. 52.

[13] The description which follows of the various branches of USIA was taken from *Agency,* pp. 1-22, discussion with USIA personnel and a number of press releases, mostly dated Feb. 1962, describing each service of the USIA, and kindly supplied the authors by USIA.

[14] Dizard, *op. cit.,* pp. 48-68.

[15] USIA Report dated December 4, 1961. These figures may be out of date by the time this book is published. They are included only to indicate the scale of VOA's operation.

[15a] Norman Cousins notes that this distorted viewpoint is frequently the fault of Americans themselves who turn their worst face forward to foreign visitors, whose initial picture of America is far from a healthy one. In other words, visitors from overseas are exposed *first* to our lurid magazines on display at newsstands, our sensational motion picture theaters and our trashy paperback books, and only later to our finer and more human qualities. See the editorial in the Saturday Review, December 15, 1962.

[16] The directive in full. It is unsigned and undated.

[17] *Voice of America Program Schedule,* for the Middle East.

[18] Dizard, op. cit., pp. 74-76.

[19] "Background on Soviet Jamming," USIA (not dated, p. 3).

[20] *A Free Voice of the Free World,* RIAS, Berlin; pamphlet; no page number. See also Dizard, *op. cit.,* pp. 83-85.

[21] The following material was taken from the pamphlet *Cuban Crisis, 1962; USIA in Action,* United States Government Printing Office, 1962, pp. 1-7.

[22] In *Newsweek, loc. cit.*

[23] *The New York Times,* April 17, 1957.

[24] *The New York Herald Tribune,* March 10, 1962.

[25] "Communication Crisis! What Can Persuaders Do?" *Printers' Ink,* September 14, 1962, pp. 28-73.

[26] *The Commonweal,* Sept. 18, 1959, pp. 517-518.

[27] *The Commonweal,* December 11, 1959, pp. 322-324.

[28] *The New York Times,* Sept. 24, 1961.

[29] *Department of State Bulletin,* Feb. 6, 1961, pp. 182-195.

CHAPTER 10

[1] *New York Times,* April 24, 1962 in a speech delivered at the annual luncheon of the Associated Press.

[2] Franz M. Joseph (ed.) *As Others See Us,* Princeton, N.J.: Princeton University Press, 1959, p. 105.

[3] Quoted in Virginius Dabney, "How the World Sees the United States," *Saturday Review,* September 23, 1961, p. 13.

[4] Israel Zangwill, *The Melting Pot.*

[5] One writer remembers clearly a lengthy and powerful World War II training film, the sole objective of which was to undo the American ideal of fair play for the G.I.'s training for combat. "The other side doesn't play fair," it said in effect, "so forget your American orientation." That so ephemeral a concept as "fair play" should be deemed by the military worthy of attention in the training of our citizen Army is an interesting comment on our values.

[6] See, for instance, Max Ways, "The Confused Image America Presents," *Life Magazine,* October 5, 1959, pp. 157-172, as good an example as any of this trend.

[7] These discontents weave aplenty in such highbrow compendia on American culture as Bernard Rosenberg and David M. White, *Mass Culture,* Glencoe, Illinois: The Free Press, 1957 and Chandler Brossard *The Scene Before You,* New York: Rinehart and Co., 1955 and others.

[8] Max Lerner, *America as a Civilization,* New York: Simon and Schuster, 1957, pp. 55-73.

[9] One British humorist even attempted to describe what America was like even though he had never been here. The results were intended to be comic, but they were only slightly worse than efforts by some of his compatriots who have viewed us first-hand.

[10] Edward W. Chester, *Europe Views America,* Washington, D.C.: Public Affairs Press, 1962.

[11] Essay in Joseph, *op. cit.,* pp. 196-198.

[12] *The New York Times,* Sept. 25, 1961.

[13] *Ibid.,* Dec. 21, 1961.

[14] Essay in Joseph, *op. cit.,* p. 65.

[15] *Ibid.,* pp. 64ff.

[16] The authors are indebted to Professor Sidney Towne of the Department of Journalism at New York University for his observations, based on travel experience, that the USSR is a society oriented toward the coming generation, not the present one.

[17] Kayham International, Tehran, April 1962. The authors are grateful to Professor Walter Anderson, Dean of the School of Education at New York University, whose keen eyes spotted this satirical article while in Iran.

[18] See the book review of *The Other American* by Michael Harrington in the *New York Times,* March 21, 1962.

[19] *The New York Times Book Review,* Jan. 28, 1962.

[20] "Omer Celâl Sarck," in Joseph, *op. cit.,* p. 144.

[21] Marija Vilfanin, *ibid.,* pp. 128-9.

[22] Adlai E. Stevenson, "Dual Education Problem: School and Home," *The New York Times Magazine,* April 10, 1958.